Goal Setting and Procrastination

An Essential Guide to Setting Goals, Creating Action Plans, Developing Habits for Success, and Curing Laziness Once and For All

Contents

Part 1: Goal Setting

What You Need to Know About Setting Goals and How to Create Action Plans and Habits for Success that Don't Require Immense Willpower

GOAL SETTING

What You Need to Know About Setting Goals and How to
Create Action Plans and Habits for Success that Doesn't
Require Immense Willpower

DEON HILLMAN

Introduction

Do you think you get everything you want in life? Have you set goals for yourself in the past and accomplished them? Do you even know what your goals are? Don't worry if your answer is no to all these questions. You aren't alone if you are struggling with this. However, if you wish to succeed, then you must spend some time thinking about all the things you want in life.

Who doesn't want to succeed in life? Sadly, not many people know where or how to start. What differentiates the massive chunk of the general population from all those who succeed? No, it is not wealth, success, popularity, or sheer luck. The only factor that differentiates successful people from the rest is their power of choice. They consciously turned their lives around and create the future they wanted. To do this, they set goals for themselves. They not only set goals, but they ensured that they gave it their all to attain those goals.

If you put your mind to it, there is nothing you cannot achieve. All you need to do is realize what you want to achieve and then give it your all. Think of it as a slight push in the right direction. Add in some effort, and you accomplish your goals. Well, this is precisely what this book does for you.

When you set certain goals in life, you will have a sense of direction. Without a goal, you get nowhere, and procrastination will inevitably set in. A goal brings clarity and vision in life. When these things are present, you will automatically do everything to turn your goal into a reality. There are different aspects of your life you can set goals in, ranging from your personal to professional life. Setting and attaining goals need not be a complicated process. It all starts with understanding who you are and what you want in life. Once you identify your core values and beliefs, it becomes easier to understand who you are. When you know who you are, it becomes easier to develop goals in sync with your core values. Don't worry if all this seems a little scary right now. After you go through the information in this book, setting and attaining goals will seem quite doable.

In this book, you will learn about the meaning of setting goals, the benefits it offers, personality traits and goals, the pitfalls of SMART goals, and how to attain your goals. You will also learn to identify your mission, vision, and core values, while furthering the understanding of your goals using "WHY" and "HOW" you want to attain them. Besides all this, you will learn about simple hacks for lazy goal setting, mind mapping, the power of vision boards, time management, and tips to attain your goals. When you learn to identify obstacles or mistakes in goal setting, it becomes easier to take corrective action. This book also provides information about the importance of focus, motivation, and self-discipline. This book is your one-stop guide to setting and attaining goals.

By creating actionable plans and learning good habits, you can attain your goals, even if you lack willpower and motivation. To be successful, all that you need to do is follow the information in this book. So, if you are ready to learn more about all this, then let us get started without further ado.

Chapter One: So Why Set Goals?

What are Goals?

Take a moment and try to answer this question, "What do you want in life?" Think about all the things you wish to attain. It's quite likely that you will be able to list various things like leading a happy and successful life, carving a successful career, maintaining good relationships, improving your bank balance, and so on. Usually, most of us have brilliant ideas, but these ideas are never materialized. At the smallest sign of inconvenience, an inexperienced risk-taker convinces himself that it is the end of the world, and he will retreat.

Once you pursue your goals, you will be in a place where taking sensible risks becomes easier. Unless you take risks, you accomplish nothing in life. When you take a risk, you must prepare yourself to be criticized and even prepare yourself to second-guess whatever decision you make. While understanding any resistance to the goals you have set, think about the different things that can go wrong and be flexible enough to overcome any objections to your adopted approach. Who doesn't want to succeed? However, there are two essential qualities many people lack, and these are patience and persistence. It is where goals come into the picture.

A goal is a specific and quantifiable objective you wish to attain within a given timeframe. There is a direct and strong correlation between the effort you make to achieve them and realizing the goal with goals. Unlike a dream or a wish, mostly based on wishful thinking and sheer luck, goals can be easily divided into short-term objectives that become checkpoints to ensure you are on the right track. Therefore, a goal is the aim of specific action to attain a predefined standard of proficiency within a specific timeframe. It helps you understand the level of competence you wish to attain while creating useful parameters to measure your current performance.

What is Goal Setting?

Goal setting is a conscious process you undertake to attain goals. The importance of setting a goal and the entire process of setting goals must never be overlooked. The way your life turns out depends on how you choose goals and the way you perceive them. If you go about life with a passive attitude, you cannot accomplish anything. The goal-setting theory is based on a simple idea that conscious goals determine your action and that your individual goals influence conscious human behavior. To simplify it, goal setting helps you decide what is good for your welfare and then prompts you to realize those goals through conscious action.

Whenever you ask the question, "What is goal setting?" remember that goals differ from one person to another. A variety of factors ranging from lifestyle to values and your definition of success define your goals. Therefore, your goals will be unique to you, and don't be bothered if they are not like someone else's goals. The classic definition of goal setting essentially comes down to a simple process of identifying something you wish to attain and then defining various measurable objectives and a timeframe to achieve that objective. There are different areas where you can set goals. You can set financial goals, lifestyle goals, health goals, fitness goals, and so on. Learning to set goals in different areas of your life makes it easier to accomplish your desired outcome.

Principles of Setting Goals

There are certain principles upon which goals are based. In this section, let us look at the different principles of goal setting.

Commitment

Your attachment to the goal and the degree of determination to attain it, despite facing obstacles, is known as commitment. The chances of attaining your goals significantly increase when you are committed to them. If you discover that your performance level is less than optimum, then commitment to the goal ensures that you have the inherent motivation to adjust your performance to attain the goal. When you are not committed, especially when it comes to challenging goals, the chances of giving up on the goal increase. After all, we are more inclined toward doing things we intend to accomplish. Various factors influence one's commitment levels. The desirability of a goal and the ability to attain it are the primary factors influencing your commitment level. If you want to be successful, you must possess an inherent desire and a thorough understanding of all required for attaining your goals.

Clarity

The goals you set for yourself must be clear. If the goal is vague, then the motivational value associated with it is relatively low. Setting clear, unambiguous, and precise goals ensures you can measure your progress. When the goal is clear, you better understand all the tasks you must accomplish to attain the goals.

Challenge

Regardless of the goal you set for yourself, ensure that it is attainable but is also challenging. Your performance improves when you tackle a challenging goal. It, in turn, improves your levels of self-satisfaction and motivation to find suitable strategies to unlock your potential. If the goal you set is unattainable, it will merely make you feel unsatisfied and even frustrated.

Complexity

Task complexity is another principle you must adhere to while setting goals. If the goal is complicated or out of your skillset's purview, it can become overwhelming. It can harm your productivity, morale, and motivation to attain the goal. The time limit you set to attain a goal must be realistic. Giving yourself sufficient time to attain a goal provides opportunities for reassessing the goal's complexity while enabling you to improve your performance. Even if you are motivated, you can become overwhelmed if the goal is complicated for your existing skillset.

Feedback

Feedback, whether or not it is internal or external, helps determine your progress and how much the goal has been accomplished. An unambiguous system of feedback ensures the desired action is taken whenever necessary. If your performance is below the required performance needed to attain a goal, feedback gives you a chance to reflect upon the progress you make. When you do this, it becomes easier to take corrective action.

Benefits of Setting Goals

The first step toward turning any of your dreams into reality is through establishing specific goals. In this section, let us look at some of the benefits you can reap by setting goals for yourself.

Measuring Your Progress

You can track no progress you make unless you have a specific goal in mind. Tracking and measuring the progress you make is gratifying and self-satisfactory. Whenever you see you are moving in the right direction and are a step closer to attaining your goal, it gives you the motivation required to keep going. It helps you stay focused, keep a level head, and feel energized. For instance, let us assume that your goal is to run 10 miles. If you aren't aware of your starting point or the destination you want to reach, it becomes difficult to track how long these 10 miles will be. If you aren't aware of the time taken to reach the destination, tracking any progress you make becomes exceedingly difficult. In the same situation, if you had a specific route and time frame in mind, then you can easily track and measure the progress you make. Every mile you run brings you a step closer to attaining your goals. Goals also ensure that your motivation levels stay high. At times, it becomes easy to feel discouraged when you haven't attained a goal. In such situations, if you can see all the progress you made, you will instantly feel better about yourself.

Provides Focus

Without a specific goal in mind, any effort you make will feel disjointed and confusing. If you are unsure of what you are trying to achieve, it can cause wasted time and effort. Time and effort are two precious resources you cannot afford to squander in life. Have you ever seen a hummingbird take flight? It often looks erratic, unfocused, and confusing. Without a goal, this is pretty much how you go about your life. Now, have you seen a hawk swoop down and catch its prey? When you have a goal, your focus becomes concentrated, and you can divert all your resources toward attaining your goals. After all, all the resources are finite, and their uses are infinite. A goal helps prioritize and then shift all your focus toward attaining them. It enables you to make the most of all the resources and opportunities available to you.

Motivation Levels

When you have no goals in mind, it is easy to put off work until a later date. For instance, if an athlete knows he needs to get in shape for a specific event, he will work out every day. Whether or not he feels good about it or not, he must keep working out and exercising to ensure that he attains his goals. He will keep working toward his goals even when he feels tired or sore. He will do this because he knows he needs to get in shape for a specific event. If he had no idea of an exact destination in his mind, then what would motivate him to keep working out? Why would he want to work out when he doesn't feel like it? To avoid all this, it is quintessential that you set specific goals for yourself.

Improve Productivity

Whenever you attain a goal or accomplish it, it makes you feel successful. Once you get the taste of success, you will want to keep experiencing it repeatedly. It gives you the motivation to push yourself harder and toward the next rung of the success ladder. It enables you to challenge yourself to shatter the glass ceiling and try to accomplish even more. When you work toward attaining and surpassing the goals you set for yourself, you can achieve more than you ever thought was possible.

Overcome Procrastination

Procrastination is something we all tend to indulge in occasionally. Regardless of how motivated you are toward attaining the goal, procrastination creeps in. Whenever you set a goal, you must always establish a timeframe for attaining that goal. When there is a timeframe to work within, it helps reduce the chances of procrastination. If you know you must complete five tasks within 24 hours, you can practically avoid procrastinating because you have to complete those goals. If there is no time limit to attain a goal, then it is likely that you will keep telling yourself, "I will do it later," or "I will do that tomorrow." Once procrastination gets hold of you, it becomes exceedingly difficult to take any positive action.

By setting goals, you will finally understand how dangerous procrastination can be. Whenever you waste time, it means you have wasted another hour or another day and are moving away from your goals. It enables you to rethink your stance toward attaining your goals. Also, it helps prioritize all the tasks you must accomplish to achieve the goals you have set.

Contemplation

By setting goals, you are forced to understand what you wish to attain in life. Goals help you understand what you want from yourself and life in general. A couple of simple questions you might have to answer while doing this are as follows.

- What is your desired level of income?

- What is your ideal level of success?

- What do you want your life to look like?

- What kind of financial support should you attain your goals?

- What are your dreams and aspirations?

Once you have answered these questions, you will have a specific result in mind. This result can be easily broken down into measurable and attainable goals.

All these goals ensure that you stay motivated, overcome procrastination, and concentrate on attaining your dreams. To live your best life possible, then you must set, achieve, and surpass your goals.

Chapter Two: Goals and Your Personality Type

Goal Setting and Personalities

Before you set any goals for yourself, it is crucial to determine your personality type. Goal setting is a journey that begins with you. Therefore, it is quintessential you know all the things that make you unique, how you work, and things that make you tick. Your behaviors, interests, and motivations are some factors that determine the goals you set. Since all these factors are the byproducts of your personality, you must understand yourself before setting any goals.

Everyone is unique, so you're the only one who can understand what makes you tick. By profiling, it gives you a better insight into yourself. Take a moment and think about some successful people. How do these people usually act or behave? What are their basic traits? Do you think these traits helped them succeed? If yes, then how do you fare when you compare yourself to these people? Do you think some of your characteristics or traits are preventing you from succeeding?

Some traits are conducive to success and achievement. However, even if you don't possess them, it doesn't mean you are doomed to fail. It just means you must learn of the different characteristics that enable you to meet your goals and use them to your advantage. We all have certain characteristics that hold us back. So, it is time to turn negative traits into positive ones that can lead you toward success.

Behavioral preferences, intelligence preferences, and personal motivation are the primary personal indicators that influence what you do, how you relate to others, your chances of success, and your thinking process. We all behave differently toward different things. This natural behavior is unique to all individuals, and it influences the way you view success and failure. Your behavioral preferences essentially influence your general attitude in life. By understanding your natural behavior tendencies, you'll have a better idea of how this impacts the goals you set and your chances of attaining them. Intelligence preferences mean we are all good at various things, and it influences the goals we set for ourselves. By understanding your interests, you can determine your natural aptitude. No, this differs from an IQ test. Instead, you are merely trying to determine your primary aptitude. If the goal you set is not in sync with your natural aptitude, it becomes challenging to work toward achieving it. We all have different factors that motivate us. Some of these factors are inherent to our personality, while others are based on life situations. Understanding your personal motivations is quintessential to determine whether you can attain a goal or not.

Now, it is time to understand who you are as an individual and its implications. For setting your goals and working toward becoming successful, there are various self-assessment tests available online. It hardly takes a couple of minutes to complete one of these tests. The most popular personality indicator test is the Myers Briggs Personality test.

Determining the Personality Type

According to the Myers Briggs personality test, every personality type can be described using four-letter codes, such as INFP, ESTJ, ESFP, etc. Each specific letter signifies a critical aspect of the individual's overall personality. This theory suggests that even seemingly random variations in an individual's behavior are usually predictable. These variations occur due to specific differences in how individuals approach different functions like thoughts, interaction, and behavior. All these individual differences can be combined by using the Myers Briggs personality dichotomies. Each class of dichotomies consists of different and opposing styles of personality, like introversion versus extraversion. Let us understand more about the four dichotomies.

- Sensing (S) vs. Intuition (N) - This dichotomy describes how an individual absorbs information.

- Extraversion (E) vs. Introversion (I) - This dichotomy describes how individuals obtain their personal energy.

- Thinking (T) vs. Feeling (F) - This dichotomy describes how individuals tend to make decisions.

- Judging (J) vs. Perceiving (P) - This dichotomy describes how an individual tends to organize his world.

Extraversion

Extroverts are energized whenever they spend time around others and in public settings. Such people love being the center of attention and thrive on the energy of those around them. Extroverts love to speak their minds, and they are not reserved. They are usually popular and well-liked by others. If an extrovert doesn't spend sufficient time with others, he can feel drained. They love participating in group activities and attending parties. They are enthusiastic, animated, and are termed as gregarious. An extrovert's communication style is verbal and assertive. They think more straightforwardly when expressing themselves, and they love staying in the limelight. The primary characteristics of this personality include assertiveness, talkativeness, enthusiasm, and outgoing nature.

- Do you love attending parties and working in groups?

- Do you feel invigorated whenever you interact with others?

- Do you love engaging in conversations with anyone and everyone?

- Do you have plenty of friends?

- Do you think you are easily approachable?

- Do you love sharing information about yourself?

- Do you like meeting new people?

Introversion

Individuals who lean toward introversion are often characterized by their desire to concentrate on the world within them instead of the external world. They love spending time by themselves or with a select group of individuals. They feel drained whenever they spend prolonged time in public or large groups. Deep relationships matter more than inconsequential small talk. They value quality over quantity with their friend circle. They are good at listening and always think before talking. Before they express themselves, they often spend some time and process all the information internally. The primary characteristics of this personality trait include an increased need for privacy, deliberation, and independence.

- Do you feel better when you spend time with yourself?

- Do you love spending time by yourself?

- Do you feel drained whenever you spend prolonged periods in public settings?

- Do you like keeping to yourself?

- Do you have a small friend circle?

- Do others describe you as a good listener?

Sensing

Individuals with a dominant sensing personality often stay focused in the moment. They are the individuals who love living in the moment and can be described as "here and now" people. They are highly factual and process all the information using their five senses. They are literal and concrete thinkers, enabling them to see things the way they are, instead of how they wish they should be. They like trusting only those things that are certain. Realism and commonsense are two values that sensors cannot do away with. They love indulging in ideas with practical applications. The primary characteristics of this personality trait include the ability to stay realistic, factual, and practical.

- Do you live in the moment?

- Are you always aware of your surroundings?

- Do you notice small details that others often miss?

- Do you allow your senses to guide your decision-making?

- Do others describe you as being practical?

Intuition

These individuals live in the future and are always thinking about various possibilities the world offers. All the information they process is based on impressions and patterns they notice in the information. Inspiration and imagination are significant to intuitive people. They love gathering knowledge and often read between the lines. Their inherently abstract nature enables them to see the big picture and attracts them to profound ideas or concepts. The essential traits of this personality include inventiveness, imagination, abstract thinking, and idealism.

- Do you often spend a lot of time thinking about what the future holds in store for you?

- Do you like daydreaming about how your future would be?

- Are your ideas more theoretical than practical?

- Do you see things how you wish they were supposed to be instead of how they truly are?

Thinking

These people are incredibly objective, and all their decision-making is based on facts and figures. They depend on reliable information they can see and process. Their heads guide them instead of their hearts. They judge situations and the world around them based on their logic. They always value the truth over tact and can quickly notice any flaws that others don't. They are critical thinkers who love taking an objective approach toward solving a problem. However, it doesn't mean these people are devoid of emotions. The basic characteristics of this trait include the ability to stay logical, objective, rational, critical, and impersonal.

- Do you always decide with your head?

- Do you always seek the truth, regardless of its consequences?

- Do others describe you as thick-skinned?

- Are you firm with people?

Feeling

Unlike the thinking personality, these people are subjective. Most of their decision-making is based on values and principles. They use their hearts instead of their heads for making decisions. They judge situations, others, and the world based on the circumstances and their feelings. They like being appreciated and always aim to please others. Harmony and empathy are more important than any other trait for these individuals. This trait's basic characteristics include the ability to be gentle, warm, empathetic, and passionate.

- Do you hate conflict?

- Do you always decide with your heart?

- Do your emotions drive all your decisions?

- Do you consider what others might feel because of your decisions?

- Do you get hurt rather easily?

Judging

These individuals love order and organization in all aspects of their lives. They are often termed *sequential thinkers.* They love living their lives according to schedules and structures. They enjoy seeking closure and completing all the tasks they start. They love working with deadlines and take them seriously. Unless they complete their work, they cannot indulge in anything else. The judging preference doesn't mean they are judgmental. It merely refers to how an individual deals with his daily activities. The basic characteristics of this personality include control, organization, structure, and decisiveness.

- Are you good at completing all the tasks you start?

- Do you like staying organized and like sticking to schedules?

- Do you often complete tasks quickly?

- Do you complete one plan and only then move onto the next plan?

- Do you like ensuring that all the tasks you start will reach a logical conclusion?

Perceiving

The perceiving preference makes an individual flexible and adaptable. They love keeping their options open and are random thinkers. They thrive when there is no fixed schedule and love the unexpected. They usually multitask and are spontaneous. They love starting tasks more than completing them. Deadlines are usually suggestions for them, and they indulge in plenty of procrastination. They love to play while they work. This personality's basic characteristics include adaptability, spontaneity, flexibility, and a relaxed attitude toward life.

- Are you carefree and spontaneous?

- Do you hate routines and schedules?

- Do you usually procrastinate?

- Do you often have a change of heart while completing tasks?

- Do you flit from one task to another?

- Do you like keeping your options open?

Setting Goals Based on Personality Types

There are four dichotomies, and by using permutations and combinations, you will end up with 16 primary types of personalities. Each personality is a 4-letter abbreviation of the primary traits discussed above. For instance, ESFP personality traits refer to an individual who leans toward extraversion, sensing, feeling, and perception instead of introversion, intuition, thinking, and judging. Likewise, an individual with an INTJ personality leans toward introversion, intuition, thinking, and judging. All the personality dichotomies are present in every individual. However, one trait is usually more dominant than the other, and this is how personalities differ.

ENTJ

Individuals with this personality trait are often ambitious, dream big, and feel happy whenever they take any action for attaining their goals. While setting goals, ensure that you allow yourself to dream big and keep planning. Even if your goal seems complex and challenging, your driven mind and basic personality traits will ensure that you keep going.

INTJ

This personality type is fond of setting goals: a logical, well-defined, and organized future appeals to the rational mind of the INTJ personality. Your logical mind will enable you to set goals and develop a plan of action to attain those goals. Besides that, you can also easily think about all the obstacles you might face to avoid the same in the future.

ENFJ

This personality type is focused. They love spending most of their time ensuring those around them are happy in the present and the future. While setting goals, don't overlook this inherent tendency you might have. Try to choose those goals that not only improve the quality of your life but help others too. If this doesn't seem possible, try choosing those goals that will not harm others. If there is any conflict of interest, your motivation to keep going might disappear, and you will feel disappointed.

INFJ

This personality type is usually averse to setting goals. They are spontaneous and are driven by their feelings. Since the feelings of right and wrong drive them, their goals can change from one moment to another. So, while setting goals, ensure that your mind and heart are in sync with the goal you have chosen. Regardless of the area of your life you are working on, ensure that your mind and heart are in complete and total alignment. If there is any conflict of interest between these two, your chances of succeeding will reduce.

ENFP

This personality type is open to exploring the world and loves new things. However, it can be slightly problematic while setting and achieving goals. They can set goals easily but usually get bored and abandon them for anything better that comes along. Therefore, ensure that you establish a couple of measures of how to stay on track. Also, your goals must completely align with your core values and beliefs.

INFP

This personality type finds setting and working toward goals rather constraining. They love change, act according to their internal desires, and don't like being tied down to a specific thing. This can become problematic while setting goals. Therefore, try to concentrate on the bigger picture whenever you set goals. By concentrating on this, you will have the desire to keep going. Also, the bigger picture must be in sync with your deepest desires.

ENTP

This personality type loves to dream big. However, the only problem is that they often have trouble staying on the right track. They love to explore, and sticking to one goal for too long doesn't appeal to them. If you are this personality type, ensure that you keep feeding your brain various distractions to ensure that you stay on the right track. If you keep thinking about one goal, you will easily get bored. So, ensure that you concentrate on all the aspects of your life while working toward the goal.

INTP

The idea or the art of setting goals doesn't come naturally to this personality type. They are dreamers and rarely have a concrete idea of the future they desire. So, setting goals can become a little tricky. However, if you develop a structured approach to attaining your goals, you can easily circumvent this problem. Ensure that the goal you are working toward is something you honestly desire and want in life. If you do this, the chances of your mind wandering while working toward a goal will reduce. You can also set up a support system to ensure that you are on the right track.

ESTJ

This personality type loves setting goals and loves the idea of successfully completing all the tasks they put their minds to. As long as your goals are practical, the chances of attaining them are high. This personality type also loves to live in the present and do things immediately.

ISTJ

Patience and determination are two key traits of this personality type. Integrity and following through is critical to this personality type. They also like working quietly and without creating a fuss about all that they have to achieve. They derive pleasure when they strike things off their to-do list.

ESFJ

This personality type loves getting things accomplished and are often task-oriented. It makes them happy to set goals and work toward attaining those goals. However, the only problem you must know is this personality type focuses a little too much on the present. So, to be successful, and attain your goals, ensure that you consider the bigger picture. Think long-term and not just the short-term while setting goals.

ISFJ

Reliability, hard-working nature, and patience are the primary characteristics of this personality type. Therefore, working toward and attaining goals is something they love doing. However, don't try to spread yourself too thin or concentrate on working on multiple goals at the same time. So, take a couple of breaks, pace yourself, and don't be in a rush. Try to keep your goals simple and concentrate on only one thing at a time.

ESFP

This personality type is seldom interested in thinking about the future or in any long-term goals. It can become tricky to set goals for yourself if you cannot see the bigger picture. Before you set any goals, spend some time trying to think about your life. Thorough self-introspection is required to understand if you are on the right track or not.

ISFP

This personality type loves freedom, autonomy, and staying in the moment. Therefore, they might have a little trouble planning the future. Ensure that whenever you set goals, they are based on taking specific actions and behaviors. If the goals seem vague, abstract, or immaterial, you will quickly lose the motivation to stay on track.

ESTP

One of the biggest problems of this personality type is that they don't like the idea of sacrificing their lives in the present to work on carving a future for themselves. It is also one reason why they quickly abandon their goals if they interfere with their present life. This personality type thrives when there are short-term and practical goals. However, they like accomplishing things. So, whenever you set goals, ensure that the long-term goal is divided into several short-term goals.

ISTP

This personality type often sets vague goals. On the plus side, they are motivated to attain the goals they set for themselves. However, they always stick to a specific aspect of their lives. To succeed in life and an all-rounder, you must set goals in all aspects of your life and not just one. So, try setting those goals that you pursue outside your comfort zone while directing you toward excellence.

Note: remember that these are mere suggestions based on the dominant traits of various personality types. The goals you set for yourself boils down to your wants and desires in life.

Chapter Three: Why You Don't Need S.M.A.R.T (or Other Fancy) Goals

A SMART goal is a commonly-used acronym to define small, measurable, attainable, realistic, and time-bound goals. SMART goals are common, and it is perhaps the first thought that pops into your head when you think about setting goals. The primary idea behind SMART goals is to come up with small yet clearly defined goals that lend direction while establishing a specific timeframe to attain the said goals. It is believed this timeline helps overcome procrastination while motivating you to stay on track. So, it is safe to assume that these goals work exceptionally well while working toward attaining a well-defined target if everything else stays the same. When the target is realistic and the progress is well within your control, these goals provide short-term direction and enable you to plan for other long-term goals.

SMART goals aren't always the ideal fit. This goal cannot be blindly applied to all pursuits in life. Doing this is the perfect recipe for disaster. If you want to achieve ultimate greatness or are aiming for big dreams, especially in an ever-changing environment, these goals are inadequate and can be detrimental to success. SMART goals are based on the assumption that the person setting them has innate willpower and motivation to attain the said goals. It might not always be the case, and it is okay if you don't set SMART goals. So, you no longer need SMART goals to attain success.

Think about an important goal you achieved. Perhaps you successfully ran a marathon, lost all the excess weight you were carrying, or maybe made a career change. Now, ask yourself these questions.

- Was that achievement easy or difficult to attain?
- Did it take little or extra effort to attain that goal?
- Did you already know everything you needed when you started, or did you have to learn new skills along the way?
- Were you completely free from worry, or did you have a couple of doubts along the way?

So, what do these questions tell you about your history with any of the significant goals in life? You will realize that every notable accomplishment in your life resulted from a challenging goal. It required a lot of effort, was tricky, you probably had to learn something new, and might even have had moments of worry. All the noteworthy accomplishments of successful people were often difficult, requiring a lot of effort, depending on their ability to learn new skills, and even resulted in some nervousness.

Now, when you look at SMART goals, you will realize all that's stated above is quite the opposite of what SMART goals suggest. Steve Jobs used to say, "We are here to put a dent in the universe." Well, you cannot put a dent in the universe if you keep doing things entirely attainable. With SMART goals, it almost looks like it says, "Play it safe and stick within your limits." If you get stuck in your comfort zone, you cannot succeed. If you keep working to attain only the things you know you can do easily, you cannot discover true greatness. If every goal is realistic and attainable, then different inventions we see today like the Kindle, the Internet, the iPod, the Human Genome Project, etc., would not exist. SMART goals stifle creativity, and they aren't the key to dreaming big. If your dreams are confined to only things you can accomplish, you can never push yourself to your limits or even discover your true potential.

Fortunately, most of us have plenty of undiscovered potentials stored within. To get there, then you need challenging goals, and SMART goals will not work. In this section, let us look at some reasons SMART goals don't always work.

Measuring Success and Failure

While using the acronym SMART, the goal you set must be measurable and specific. These two criteria help objectively evaluate whether you have achieved a specific goal or not. This type of goal is quite useful while managing progress. However, their effectiveness is based on another factor: whether the environment you are working in is static or dynamic. SMART goals work only in a controllable environment. Therefore, applying this criterion to measure failure or success, especially in a dynamic or extreme environment, can be demotivating. Also, it might motivate you in the wrong direction. This outcome is potentially dangerous and detrimental to success.

By measuring success using SMART goals, you might end up where you are blindly pursuing your goals. You might not even realize why you are doing certain things, just because you are trying to accomplish your set goals. In such a situation, if you fail to meet a SMART goal, it can be quite demotivating. So, if your goal is to complete writing a 200-page book within a week, failing to meet this goal will essentially demotivate you. When you set this goal, you were probably sure that you could complete it. However, if you don't complete this within the set timeframe, you can feel lost. Because of this goal, you might not even be able to see the progress you have made. Instead of appreciating all that you have achieved, you will concentrate only on the objective you did not meet. So, the factor that gives you the motivation to keep going will send you into a tailspin when you don't achieve the established goals.

Narrows Your Focus

When you fixate all your attention only on one SMART goal, then you will ignore everything else. You might be so overcome by the need to attain this goal that it becomes your only priority. This fine-tuned approach to attaining a goal will work in a steady-state situation. Well, life is unpredictable, and it is improbable that factors that might influence your ability to attain the goal will always stay the same. In your bid to accomplish the SMART goal, you might overlook all the other opportunities that come along your way.

Giving Up Quickly

At times, SMART goals can be a little discouraging before or after attaining the goals. Were there times when you said, "I don't have the time to this," while excusing yourself for not doing something that you planned to do on a specific day? Well, the most popular application of the SMART goal is time management. Whenever it comes to time allocation for a specific task, it is usually in terms of all or nothing thinking. SMART goals are often viewed as a singular entity. So, if you cannot do something that you planned, it can be discouraging, and it might increase the **chances of abandoning the goal altogether.**

Low Goals

When you start using SMART goals to test whether your goals are the most effective or not, you are essentially encouraging yourself to set lower goals. Specific and measurable goals are ideal in certain situations, but usually, they produce results that lead to premature satisfaction or even reduced effort. For instance, let us assume that a salesperson sets a goal of increasing sales in his region by 5%. Now, he achieves this goal within the set timeframe. So, were he following SMART goals, then he would be happy about achieving this target. However, if the growth potential in that region could have been increased to 15%, he will not use his full potential. In this instance, SMART goals lead to premature satisfaction. Also, he might lose enthusiasm to further increase sales since he has achieved a SMART goal.

Compromises

The first criterion in a SMART goal is that the goal must be specific. Setting a specific goal is effective. However, on the downside, there are inherent problems in setting specific goals. Perhaps the biggest trouble is, you might ignore the different factors that might help you attain your goals. For instance, during the 1970s, Ford manufactured Pintos to solely reduce the overall cost of the car to less than $2000. In their bid to do this, they cut corners. They compromised on safety and came up with a design that placed the gas tank in the car in a position that left it vulnerable in cases of collisions. It not only resulted in several claims against the company but also cost them their reputation. By using SMART goals, the company attained its objective of reducing the overall cost but ended up making a hefty compromise on the safety of the vehicle. Likewise, when you set SMART goals, you open up yourself for unnecessary compromises since your primary focus will be on a specific goal.

Can be Misleading

Before pursuing an achievable and realistic goal like concentrating on your next promotion, increasing your sales, or getting an award, ask yourself, "At what cost am I doing this?" You might not realize it, but you can easily overload yourself with several top priorities by setting SMART goals. A specific task is a top priority for a reason. So, when too many tasks vie for this position, the position itself becomes meaningless. Everything cannot occupy the number one position on your list of priorities.

When you observe every goal in isolation, it might seem achievable and realistic within a given timeframe. This might prompt you to become overly ambitious and believe that you can figure a way out and fit everything in your schedule. However, remember that "realistic" is a very relative term, and it is not absolute. It is not just about understanding whether a specific goal is realistic, given your capabilities, but also about understanding how realistic it is in relation to your other goals. You need to have a broad vision if you want to pursue lofty dreams and goals. SMART goals merely act as checkpoints, but they must not be the end goal.

Can Be Overwhelming

It can be a source of incredible stress if you are continually working toward attaining specific and time-bound goals. We already lead stressful lives and don't need any external or added stress. It can harm your health and even your overall lifestyle. Keep in mind that pursuing a long-term goal is not a short journey. It is something that you must keep doing consistently. It takes plenty of focus and energy. If you set SMART goals for yourself, you are merely increasing the stress you feel.

So, you no longer have to spend hours on end coming up with SMART goals. It is time to look for more effective and efficient techniques of goal setting.

Chapter Four: Your Mission, Vision, and Core Values

Usually, the terms vision and mission statement are used while describing the purpose of an organization. However, there is no reason why you cannot create your personal mission and vision statements.

So, you must be wondering why you need any of these statements. Well, words tend to have a certain power. When you don't have a precise long-term goal in your mind, you tend to become reactive instead of being proactive in life. Most of us usually concentrate on immediate or short-term goals whenever we make a decision. However, if you want to be successful, you must concentrate on the present and think about the future. A successful person knows this. It is one reason why most successful people often have their mission and vision statements in place.

While going through life, it is relatively easy to get overwhelmed by different mundane activities. When you have a vision statement on hand, it gives you a better idea of the future you wish to create for yourself. It also lends meaning to various activities you partake in. Apart from all this, these statements help determine your personal values and core principles that you would not want to compromise on. When you have an idea of all this, it becomes easier to set goals for yourself *and accomplish the goals.* It lends a sense of balance to your life while preventing any burnout.

By having vision and mission statements, you can become more determined. It enables you to push yourself beyond your boundaries and step outside the comfort zone. Unless and until you do this, you cannot be successful. It enables you to build a life by design and not one that occurs by chance.

In this section, you will learn about the difference between a mission statement, vision statement, and core values. Even though all these three things sound quite similar, there are minute differences between them. Once you understand these differences, it becomes easier to establish goals for yourself. Apart from this, it will also give you better insight into yourself.

Vision Statement

A vision statement usually describes a specific dream; the organization wishes to achieve. It addresses the primary question, "What is the long-term goal of this organization?" Some of the popular vision statements of different companies are as follows.

• Ford Motors - To become the world's leading consumer company for automotive products and services.

• Disney - To make people happy.

• Amazon - Our vision is to be Earth's most consumer-centric company; to build a place where people can come to find and discover anything they want to buy online.

The definition of a vision statement that applies to a company is applicable on a personal level too. Your vision statement essentially describes one long-term goal that you wish to achieve in your life. It is also a true reflection of all the different values or characteristics that are dear to you. Here is an example of a personal vision statement, "I want to be a successful politician. It is my vision to inspire, motivate, and encourage people to live their lives to their fullest potential while contributing to society's development."

Mission Statement

A mission statement often describes how an organization wishes to attain its vision. The same rule applies to a personal mission statement too. It essentially addresses the question, "What can I do to attain your goals?" A vision statement deals with the future you want to carve for yourself.

On the other hand, a mission statement deals with the action you can take today to create the future. It provides a sense of direction and ensures that all your actions will bring you closer to your goal. It also prevents distractions from creeping in, which hinders your ability to concentrate on your goals.

Core Values

Your core values are different characteristic traits, beliefs, and principles that support your vision and mission statements. Some certain beliefs or principles are non-negotiable under any circumstances. They are quintessential for ensuring that your personal satisfaction stays high while you concentrate on attaining your goals. Different examples of core values include acceptance, logic, growth, safety, justice, knowledge, faith, passion, adventure, etc. Unless your goals align with your mission and vision statement, the chances of attaining them aren't high. If your goals contradict these things, you will quickly lose interest in them and might start procrastinating.

Steps to Follow

Here is a simple template you can follow in coming up with your mission statement. You don't have to spend hour's together brainstorming ideas. Start answering the questions as you go along, and within no time, you will have your personal mission statement. It doesn't take long to answer these questions, so set some time aside for it. Also, ensure that you are answering the questions as truthfully and honestly as you possibly can. After all, the aim is to develop your personal vision and mission statements.

Your Basic Characteristics

Here are various personal characteristics, and it is time to start prioritizing them from the most to the least important ones. If you think a characteristic is missing, feel free to add it to the list.

- Capable
- Broadminded
- Ambitious
- Dependable
- Cheerful
- Courageous
- Forgiving
- Friendly
- Honest
- Imaginative
- Helpful
- Intellectual
- Logical
- Independent
- Loving
- Organized
- Polite
- Obedient
- Innovative
- Self-confident
- Self-assured
- Self-controlled

What Are Your Values?

Here are various personal values, and it is time to start prioritizing them from the most to the least important ones. If you think something is missing, feel free to add it to the list. Carefully rank them because these values will act as guiding principles in your life.

- Creating a comfortable life
- Attaining personal and professional goals
- Leading an exciting life
- Living a happy life
- Desiring family security
- Peace of mind
- A sense of accomplishment
- Forming meaningful relationships
- Contributing to society
- A pleasurable life
- Spiritual salvation
- Leaving a legacy
- Happiness and independence

What is Important?

Carefully go through the ranking of the different personal characteristics and values you completed in the previous sections. Were there any values or characteristics that are important to you but weren't listed? If yes, then you merely need to add them to your list. Now, start rating them in their order of importance. Start listing out eight of your topmost values and characteristics. All these will be your core values and characteristics that you cannot swerve from in any situation.

- List your values

- List your characteristics

What Roles Do You Play?

We all tend to play different roles in life like that of a student, employee, son, daughter, grandparent, husband, wife, parent, manager, CEO, etc. Think about all the different roles you play and start describing the purpose you serve in a specific role. There are four specific questions you must answer while listing out the rules and your purpose in it. The questions are as follows.

- Why do you play this role?

- Why is this role important to you?

- Is there anyone who depends on you? If yes, then who depends on you?

- Who benefits from all these roles?

Note: Don't list out more than five roles.

How Do You Interact With Others?

You cannot get along in this world unless you get along with people and interact with them. There are various ways in which we successfully interact with others. In this section, it is time to list how you interact with others. Here are specific examples you can use. If something is missing from the list, please feel free to add on.

- Entertain

- Advice

- Reassure

- Teach

- Lead

- Manage

- Encourage

- Educate

- Love
- Stimulate
- Motivate
- Inspire
- Help
- Stud
- Plan
- Sell
- Provide
- Excite
- Support
- Serve

What About Awards?

- If you ever won an award, what would the award be for?
- How would you want the presenter to introduce you?
- What would your loved ones want to hear from you?
- What do you want in life?
- What do you want people to say about you after ten years?
- What do you want to accomplish in life?
- What experiences do you want to have?
- What do you want to own in life?

Time To Visualize

Now it is time to start visualizing your idea of a perfect world. What does your idea of a perfect world look like? Don't be judgmental, and allow your imagination to guide your way. Don't criticize yourself and merely make a mental note of all your thoughts. Once you do this, start listing out your idea of a perfect world.

Summing It All Up

Once you have completed all the different steps mentioned until now, you will better understand yourself. You will know your core values and basic characteristics. Combine all the concepts and words you picked up from the list of values, characteristics, roles, interactions, and things you want in life, along with your idea of a perfect world. When you combine all this, you'll be left with your mission statement. A simple example of a personal mission statement would be, "The purpose of my life is to use all the skills at my disposal to teach and motivate others to understand the journey in life and enjoy it."

Additional Tips

Your vision and mission statement must not exceed 50 words each. These statements must be easy to understand, concise, and reflect your true values and purpose. Also, don't fear making your vision statement bold. However, don't forget to be a little realistic. These statements must be in sync with your personal and professional goals. There are three crucial questions your vision and mission statements must address, and they are as follows.

- What are your passions in life?

- What are your core values?

- What sets you apart from the rest of the world?

Remember that a good vision statement often inspires you and pushes you to live your life to the fullest. It enables you to zero in on your passions and make the most of your skills and resources.

Once you have successfully created your vision and mission statements, don't forget to review them. Yes, they are usually long-term in nature, but it doesn't mean they are set in stone. As you go through life, different things will change. Therefore, your vision and mission statements must also change accordingly. Keep reviewing them and give yourself the required flexibility to modify them according to different circumstances. As you go along, there will be changes in your family life, job, career, health, and so on. Therefore, revise them at least once every year and try to accommodate all the changes.

Chapter Five: Pinpointing Your Goals with Why's and How's

Do you ever think about your personal reason for waking up every day? Unless you identify your purpose, it will become difficult to set any goals for yourself. In the previous chapters, you were given information about defining your vision statement, mission statement, and core values. However, these things will not hold any significant meaning to you unless you understand your reasons for setting goals. In this section, you'll learn about three simple steps you can follow to understand your purpose and identify the right goals along the way.

- Start by asking yourself "WHY" you want to attain specific goals.

- Now, ask yourself "HOW" you can implement your core values.

- It is time to ask yourself, "WHY" you must implement your core values.

Step #1: What is Your WHY?

Importance of Having a "WHY."

Unless you understand your purpose or "WHY," you cannot pursue things in life that give you absolute fulfillment, your reasons often serve as a point of reference for all the actions you take and decisions you make. It enables you to measure your progress and understand when you have attained your goals. There is a term in Japanese "ikigai" that translates to "a reason for being." Unless you know your purpose, you cannot make your life worthwhile.

When you understand your "WHY," it brings about a sense of clarity; if you ever noticed all people with a strong sense of purpose, they are often unstoppable. They have the power to shape their lives and live the way they want to. Likewise, when you have specific goals you wish to achieve and know your reasons for doing the same, you have a purpose every morning. If you don't know this purpose, you will waste your precious time and energy doing things that hold little or no meaning to you. Your purpose also ensures that you will follow up on your goals.

If you don't like settling for less, you must have a purpose you wish to work toward; when your passion fuels your goal, your chances of success increase. It also ensures that you stay focused on all the goals you have established. When you know what truly matters to you in life, you can dedicate your limited resources to those things. It is also a great way to de-clutter your life. If you are unaware of what is important, you might expend your limited energy on unnecessary clutter.

Setbacks are quite common in life. Unless you have a strong sense of purpose for attaining a specific goal, you cannot overcome setbacks. A lack of purpose will make you view a setback as the end of the road. A setback is merely an opportunity to learn and grow. You cannot think like this only when you have a strong sense of purpose. Therefore, your "WHY" enables you to develop resilience. Resilience allows you to bounce back from adversities.

When you know your purpose and understand what matters to you, you can hold onto your values. Therefore, having and understanding your reasons for attaining a goal enables you to live your life with integrity. When you follow your core values and stick to your primary characteristics, you will feel more satisfied with yourself and your life.

Steps to Find Your "WHY."

Now that you understand the importance of your "WHY," it is time to find your "WHY."

Make a list of all the activities you used to enjoy but don't indulge in anymore. When having fun, time certainly passes more quickly. So, it is time for a little self-introspection to identify your passions. Unless you are passionate about your goals, you cannot attain them. When you follow your passions, you can ensure that all your energy, time, and resources are spent working on something that lends meaning to your life. Another simple way to do this is to remember all the things you used to do in your childhood just because it was fun. As you go down memory lane, you might notice specific patterns or trends in activities you enjoy. Think about it for a moment, and these patterns hold clues to your real purpose in life.

Most adults often lose touch with various things they loved as children. Sadly, in adulthood, most of us falsely believe we must do things only when we are rewarded for them. This transactional nature of existence imbibed into us by societal norms can make anyone feel dejected. Therefore, it is time to put a stop to all this and understand your passions.

In sync with the previous step, it is time to think about all the things you would want to do in life, even if it made you look like a fool. Before you can excel at something, there will; be some point you stumble and fall because of a lack of competence and knowledge. You cannot keep working on something even after embarrassing yourself for making mistakes unless you are passionate about it. Unless the activity at hand is meaningful to you, you will give up at the first sign of trouble. So, think about things you wouldn't shy away from, even if it means feeling foolish or silly.

Now, it is time to understand your talents. Not a lot of us know all our talents. Most of us brush away our talents because they don't seem worthy of societal acceptance. A simple way to understand yourself better is by noticing what others ask of you when they need your help. You might not be able to see your talents how others do. For instance, you might not realize that you are inspiring your siblings, colleagues, or friends to be more like you. What is one thing your friends always thank you for? Do they come to you for advice? Do you serve as a sounding board? Another simple way to do this is by asking your loved ones about what they think your strengths are. Identifying your strengths can also enable you to find your passion in life. Once you identify your passion, setting goals becomes more manageable.

No one likes thinking about death. No one likes believing life is short, and most of us avoid these thoughts. Even if it sounds morose, it is time for critically analyzing your life. What would you do if you knew you just had a year to live? Would you keep living the life you are living right now? Or would you want to make any changes? We are all used to thinking, "I can do this later." However, what would you do if you knew that you just had a year to do everything you ever wanted and wished for? It helps put things in perspective and give you a better understanding of yourself. It will also give you a better sense of purpose.

The best way to determine your purpose in life is by identifying things you can do to enrich others' lives. It would help if you had a certain degree of self-awareness to do this. When you are grateful for the life you live and contribute toward others' wellbeing, you will be more satisfied with yourself. It, in turn, will give you a strong sense of purpose.

What are the different things in life for which you wouldn't mind going the extra mile? There will be things you would want to keep making an effort even after facing setbacks and failures. Many people fail to realize that passion is only the result of action instead of causing it. If you are complacent, you can never find your passion in life. Finding your passion is a process of trial and error. If you're not willing to go out of your way for something, then it means you're not passionate about it.

To sum it all up, here are questions you must answer to find your "WHY."

- What do you love the most?
- What means the most to you in life?
- What would you want to do if you just had a year to live?
- What would you go out of your way for?
- What are the different activities you enjoy?
- What can you do to enrich the lives of those around you?
- What is the one thing you would love to do even if you get no monetary returns from it?

Step #2: How to Implement Your Core Values

Once you have identified your "WHY," it is time to work on your core values. Unless you implement your core values in your daily life, you cannot become successful. Your core values serve as a homing beacon. They help you identify any opportunities that come along your way while avoiding any trouble. In this section, let us look at simple tips you can follow to implement your core values.

You can revisit the previous chapter to understand your core values once again. They usually are single words or simple phrases. Once you have a list of your top 10 core values, write them down on post-its, and you can place them in your home. You can also digitize them and use them as screensavers, the home screen on your desktop, or place it anywhere else where you will see it daily.

When you keep glancing at it daily, this message gets embedded in your mind.

Another great way to ensure that your core values always stay in your mind is by discussing them with your loved ones. When your close circle knows your core values and regularly discusses them, these values get stuck in your subconscious. It also enables them to get a better understanding of you as an individual.

The company you keep matters a lot. Regardless of your age, your company defines your personality. You might not realize it, but a great way to manage your core values is by managing the company you keep. It doesn't mean that everyone you spend the time that must share your core values. It merely means they must fit in it. For instance, if one of your core values is creativity, it doesn't mean you have to keep looking for all those individuals who are equally creative. However, it does mean you need people around you who support your creative approach in life. Instead of bringing you down or causing conflict, your support system must encourage you. When you spend time with ambitious, happy, successful people (and all things desirable), their positive traits will positively affect you. Likewise, spending time with negative company will negatively affect you.

Your core values will enable better decision-making. Put aside a couple of minutes in the morning to list all the tasks you wish to accomplish during the day. Once you have listed all the tasks, use your core values to gauge whether the tasks at hand are important for you or not. For instance, if your core value is impact, go through your list of tasks and weed out all those tasks that don't meet this core value. You'll probably want to do all those tasks that help maximize your results, but with minimum effort. Everything you do must follow who you are. When you do this, it becomes easier to attain your goals while maintaining your personal satisfaction.

When you integrate your core values into regular conversations, they take on a whole new meaning altogether. Even casually speaking about these core values allows you to express yourself. It is also a great way to be consistent while thinking about your core values. By making a part of your regular vocabulary, you get a chance to remind yourself of all you are and what you want to do in life without overlooking or forgetting it.

Not everyone is motivated to accomplish their goals. It is true when the goals you have set for yourself are not something that you're passionate about. Therefore, it is time to use your core values as motivators. They help determine the future you want to have. Every opportunity you get and the goals you set must be based on your core values. Unless they agree on your core values, they result in unnecessary internal conflict.

To keep improving yourself, then you need to spend some time for self-introspection. Take some time and think about all the different tasks you accomplished. Give yourself a moment to understand whether the day that went by you was in tune with your core values or not. If you notice any discrepancies, you can take corrective action to ensure that you get back on track the following day.

Step #3: Revisit Your "WHY"

The final step is to revisit your "WHY." Now, it is time to question yourself about why you must implement your core values. When you go through the different questions in this section, you will realize that your core values go back to your goals. Once your goals and core values are in sync, it becomes easier to take action, stay on track, and attain the goals.

What is Your Purpose?

• The first step to ensuring that the goals you set for yourself are right for you is by asking yourself these questions.

• Why do you want to attain this goal?

- Is this goal something you want to pursue, or do you feel like you must pursue it?

- What is the core value in your life this goal caters to?

If you feel like you are forced to pursue a goal, it is not the right one. If you have set a goal you wish to pursue, keep reminding yourself why it is important.

What is Your Idea of Success?

Start with the end result and visualize that you have attained your goals. Now, think back and list out the major milestones that helped you reach your destination. By doing this, you can identify any possible obstacles you might come across while working toward your ultimate goal. It essentially helps you avoid any roadblocks or obstacles, and instead, concentrate on attaining your goals.

What Will Your Life Look Like Once You Have Attained Your Goals?

Besides the previous question, try to think about any of the additional questions you can ask yourself to clarify the things you wish to achieve in life. What are your values? Are your goals in sync with your values? Is the goal something you honestly want, or are you trying to live up to someone else's expectations? The more questions you ask yourself, the closer will you be to the right answer. Unless the goal you have set for yourself is the right one, your chances of attaining it are slim.

What is Your Superpower?

The ability to question yourself is nothing short of a superpower. Unfortunately, not many first understand its true meaning and don't use this power at all. The best way to ensure that you are heading in the right direction is to question your chosen direction. So, who are you? By answering this question, you will have a real sense of your purpose and meaning in life. Besides this, it also gives you a better understanding of your core values and the goals you have set for yourself. Besides all this, it also helps determine whether the goal you set is the right one or not. Unless your goals go back to your core values, you cannot work to succeed.

Why Did You Choose the Goal?

Will this goal change any aspect of your life? If yes, then why will this goal bring about the said change? The chances of succeeding improve when you question yourself about all the things you do in life. When you know why you are doing something, the goal becomes more straightforward and less ambiguous. If your goal is vague, then the results will be vague too. It might even make you feel like you are a failure because of all this vagueness. So, try eliminating this by asking yourself why you chose a specific goal.

What Is It That You Wish To Achieve Ultimately?

The primary idea of this question is to help identify your goals and concentrate on taking actionable steps for attaining that goal. Once you know what you want in life or different aspects of your life, you can easily develop a plan of action that leads you to the most successful outcome. Every step you take in the present and the future must align with and be a part of the bigger picture. Unless you see the bigger picture, you cannot take these steps.

What Is Your Ideal Job Description?

Most of us know all the things we don't like about our job or art lives. When we know these things, we continuously try running away from them. Instead of doing this, think about the things you like. What is your ideal job description? Once you answer this, then you have a goal you can work toward. Instead of running away from it, you can run toward the goal you want to achieve. It also enables you to stop concentrating on the pain points and work on taking steps toward your ideal job description. It ensures that you are working in the right direction.

What Are Your Values?

You will be investing plenty of your resources to attain a goal. Your goal is closely associated with your core values. Unless you have clarity about your core values, you cannot attain your goals. Concentrate on things important to you and in-line with your goals. It helps reduce any distractions while improving your chances of success. Besides this, it is also rather fulfilling when you work on things you value in life.

What Keeps You Going In Life?

To identify whether the goal you have set for yourself is the right one or not, you must start by understanding yourself. Until you know what keeps you going in life, it will become challenging to determine whether you are headed in the right direction or not. Therefore, start by understanding who you are and where you wish to go from there. Then, question yourself about why you want to do a specific thing and what you can achieve by working toward the goal.

What Do Your Loved Ones Say About Your Goal?

Even when you are confident of the things you love in life, it doesn't hurt to get a second opinion. Remember that you are merely consulting and not seeking the answers to your questions from others. You can always ask your trusted friends, family members, partner, or anyone you love to share their opinions about what they feel about your goals. It helps improve your self-awareness. Also, they might see certain opportunities and obstacles you are oblivious to. Additional information always comes in handy.

Chapter Six: Nine Lazy Goal-Setting Hacks

Are there days when you feel incredibly inspired to get your life organized? It could be a random burst of motivation at three in the morning or a constant urge to get it together after a motivating day at work. Well, if yes, then you are like the rest of us. However, there is only one small problem with this entire thing: the lack of motivation. You might experience a random burst of motivation, but you don't always feel motivated to set and work toward attaining goals. So, how can you set goals when you feel a little lazy or low on motivation? Well, in this section, you'll learn about specific practical tips you can follow to get things done quite easily.

Tip #1: Always Start Small

When you're trying to work toward a goal, start with something small. It could be a small step, but it still counts. For instance, if your goal is to get a promotion at work, it is an important goal. This goal might seem complicated and even overwhelm you. Instead of concentrating on getting promoted, concentrate on turning in all your work on time. Let others see you are dependable and punctual. Don't forget to deliver on your promises, and whenever possible, turn in the work earlier than expected. Within no time, your boss will notice the effort you make. Break down the primary goal into smaller steps you can work on. This works exceptionally well when running low on motivation.

It might sound like a SMART goal idea, but it works. However, ensure that the goal you are working toward is something you genuinely care for.

Tip #2: Talk to Others

There might be someone in your circle - a friend, family member, colleague, or acquaintance who always seem put-together and confident. If there is a go-getter in your circle, then it is time to talk with that person. Ask the person for some advice you can incorporate into your daily life and routine. You probably need not follow all the methods the other person uses, but it probably gives you better insight into the things that work and doesn't. In fact, don't merely try to copy or replicate the other person's behavior without understanding what you wish to accomplish. You might end up with some practical advice you can use to develop the kind of attitude required for succeeding.

Tip #3: Start Yesterday

If your motivation levels don't run high, or if you are not usually a motivated individual, then procrastination creeps in. Once procrastination gets hold of you, getting anything done will become incredibly difficult. Procrastination can get to the best of us. However, unless you stop procrastinating and take some action, you get nothing done. So, it is time to get started soon. Stop telling yourself, "now is not the right time," "I will do it tomorrow," or "this can wait." If you keep telling yourself these things, remember that you are merely making excuses. You are procrastinating and are putting off something until a later date, which can be done right now. If you wait, you cannot attain whatever you want. If that's not an option, then it is time to get started ASAP. If you notice procrastination creeping in while you are trying to do something, then remind yourself you were supposed to start it yesterday itself!

Time is precious, and once it goes back, you cannot get it back. So, stop wasting it and concentrate on getting things done.

Tip #4: Concentrate On Your Likes

Always concentrate on doing the things we love and forget about the rest. It might sound like a piece of advice that is easier said than done. Regardless of how much you love something, you cannot afford to forget about everything else in your life. For instance, just because you're working on a goal you desire doesn't mean you can do away with your other responsibilities like going to the grocery store, maintaining dentist appointments, and keeping up with different commitments. However, if you set a goal for yourself, then you must follow your heart and ensure there is sufficient time for it. The best way to do this is by ensuring that your goal resonates with your core values. Once you like the direction you are headed in, it becomes easier to make the required effort.

Tip #5: Understand Yourself

Accountability matters a lot when it comes to setting and attaining goals. It matters even more if you are running low on motivation or feel a little lazy. When you hold yourself accountable, not just to yourself but to others, it increases your motivation to keep going. Even when you have no motivation, the mere fact that others will hold you accountable for attaining the goal will give you the motivation to take the required action. So, whenever you set a major life goal, you can post about it on social media or talk to your close circle about it. By doing this, you are essentially telling others what you want to accomplish while making yourself more responsible for your goals. Also, it always helps to have a support system in place. Once your close circle understands what you're doing and why you are doing it, they will stand by you and give you the motivation they require on the days when you have none!

Tip #6: Not Accomplishing the Goal

At times, we all need a reality check to get started and keep moving. For attaining your goals, concentrating on the idea of success is a good idea. However, it doesn't always work. Instead, try picturing how your life would be if you don't accomplish your goals. Concentrate on how you would feel and what you would be missing out on. Concentrate on all the negative emotions associated with not attaining the goals. These negative emotions might scare you a little. Well, this is precisely what you need to keep going. A little fear is a great motivation and energy booster. The next time you don't want to work on something, remind yourself of how you would feel when you don't accomplish the goal.

Tip #7: Be Honest

Don't work on a goal merely because society tells you to or because someone in your close circle tells you to. The goal must be ideal for you, and it is time to ensure that you are not living someone else's dreams. If you are confident that you are genuinely excited and happy about something you're doing – and not just listening to those around you – then you are on the right path. If you keep doing things to please others or because others believe it is a good idea, you will never find the motivation to get things done.

Tip #8: Mini-Goals

Do you ever feel like getting someplace instead of being stuck on the side of the road, wondering how long it would take until you finally reach your destination? If this ever happens to you or has happened to you, then you'll realize it zaps out motivation. If you feel like you are not making progress, you will not want to work on it. The same stands true when you cannot see the progress you make. So, to avoid all this, it is time to set some mini-goals for yourself. Instead of getting overwhelmed, thinking about a big goal you want to achieve, concentrate on the mini-goals. For instance, if you are trying to get a promotion, then maybe you can start by getting your boss to approve one of your new ideas or maybe even spend some time connecting with your coworkers. These are relatively simple and achievable. Achievable goals will help you accomplish what seemed unattainable initially.

Tip #9: Don't Forget to Have Fun

You must put in plenty of effort to meet a specific goal. However, it doesn't mean there isn't a reason you cannot enjoy the process. If you don't enjoy doing all this, then what is the point? Even if it sounds like a cliché, meeting every challenge with a smile on your face changes the way things work out for you. Your attitude matters a lot in life. If you stay positive, understand the process, and have fun along the way, attaining goals will become more effortless.

By now, you would have realized that setting goals are not just for determined and motivated individuals. Anyone can set goals. However, the one aspect of goal setting you must not overlook is the way you set goals. If you set goals that cannot be attained or don't try to attain the goals, you will merely disappoint yourself.

Chapter Seven: Mind-Mapping for Clarity

What is Mind-Mapping?

Mind mapping is the graphic representation that helps connect information about a central topic. It is almost like a tree, where the main idea represents the trunk, and all the associations drawn from it are like the branches of a tree. In mind mapping, you can use words, pictures, or even symbols to represent your ideas and goals. Mind mapping is not a new concept, and it has been around for centuries now. Great thinkers like Leonardo da Vinci, Albert Einstein, Darwin, and even Edison used various visual representation methods to express their ideas.

The idea of mind mapping was popularized by Tony Buzan, a popular educator, author, and psychologist. To improve his ability to analyze and retain information while in college, he came up with specific keywords and phrases, adding color to essential concepts, forming associations by drawing lines, and then adding boxes to the relevant text. While doing this, he realized that the usual notes' information was noticeably less than the ones present in a mind map.

Mind mapping can be used for brainstorming, managing meetings, decision-making, organizing information, strategic thinking, improving work productivity, and even event planning. Not only students but people in many other age groups can utilize mind maps.

What Are the Benefits of Mind-Mapping?

Now that you're aware of what mind mapping means, let us look at the benefits it offers.

One of the significant benefits of mind mapping is the speed at offers. When you no longer have to write sentences and paragraphs, you can save plenty of time. All this time you saved can be used for something more creative. By merely noting down a phrase or word, you can understand the meaning of an entire sentence or paragraph. It comes in handy, especially while dealing with complicated topics, by noting down key words –or even symbols – you cut down on all the time. You might have spent making notes. It also enables your mind to form associations quickly.

Mind mapping helps improve your creativity because it emphasizes brainstorming, the formation of associations, and gradient thinking. Unlike a computer, your brain cannot function linearly, at least not all the time. Whenever you read any information, your brain undertakes various functions like comparison, integration, and synthesis of all your thoughts. Most of these mental functions rely on associations. Words are merely a verbal representation of an idea you have in your head. When you link a word to a specific idea, it helps uncover other ideas stored within. When you think about a specific topic in this manner, you might come up with various subcategories you didn't know existed, and your mind keeps forming associations all this time. It helps obtain a fresh perspective when looking at certain things in life.

A mind map is a thorough visual representation of all your ideas and thoughts in one place. Instead of going through plenty of text, you merely need to look at a mind map to get a bird's eye view of a specific topic. Processing information and understanding the same in this manner becomes easy. Also, since it is free from clutter, you save yourself plenty of trouble of having to read through a topic. Besides this, mind-mapping also allows you to look at different associations between various topics carefully.

When you start forming associations, it becomes easier for your mind to retain information. It, in turn, improves your memory. Whenever you write something down either physically on the paper or type it out on your computer, it gets stored in your memory. It is an effective way of learning when compared to reading. Mind maps are not readily available, and it takes a little effort to make them. This conscious effort you make means it is easier for your brain to remember all the information.

Since all the information and associations are represented visually, it lends a better sense of clarity. It not only offers a brief explanation or synopsis, but it ensures that you have better clarity of the subject too. A mind map doesn't encourage clattering of information, so your brain can quickly zero in on the essential concepts. Mind mapping is also a great way to brainstorm new ideas. Whenever you feel like you have hit a wall, start mind mapping. Sometimes, all it takes is to place your idea on paper or on the computer screen to help you come up with different answers to a problem.

Steps to Follow

Mind mapping is a great technique that enables you to divide your goals into smaller ones. When you make this division, you will have a better understanding of all you wish to attain. A mind map gives you a visual representation of all the small goals you can take to attain those goals in different steps. You can see all this with no excessive clutter, making it easier to understand the ideal course of action.

The first step is to collect your goals. Essentially, it means you must note different keywords or small sentences that represent your goals. Spend some time and write everything down until you cannot come up with more ideas. In this stage, you are merely dumping all your ideas on a piece of paper, and selection comes next. On a sheet of paper, write down the central theme- goals.

The next step is to start forming general associations around the central theme. For instance, the different general associations associated with goals could be various aspects of your life, like personal, professional, social, financial, or even educational. Now, go back to the list of goals you made in the previous step and segregate them according to different aspects of your life. Once you have segregated them, it is time to note all the concerned goals next to the general associations in the mind map. Once you have completed this step, you can notice different branches flowing from the central theme to different categories of goals and the subcategories in each area.

Ensure that you don't include over three goals for a specific aspect of your life. If there are more goals than this and become cluttered, the chances of getting distracted will increase. Here is a simple example of how a mind map can look. Instead of noting them in bullet points, you can place them next to one another with the central theme in the center of the page. From the central theme, draw lines until you reach the desired area of your life. It will essentially look like a cobweb spreading out in different directions. Every line you extend will merely increase the area that the web covers. You can make the mind map as detailed as you want. Under this, you can also write down the reasons for working on a specific goal and the course of action you can take to attain the goals. Use different colors to make the mind map more attractive and highlight the critical aspects of your life. However, your work doesn't, and once you have created a mind map. The mind map merely serves as a reminder of all that you wish to accomplish. So, you must put in the required effort and spend the time necessary to attain those goals.

Goals

1. Personal

a. Playing a sport you enjoy

b. Spending more time with your loved ones

c. Eating healthy and wholesome meals

2. Professional

a. Learning a specific job-related skill

b. Working for a promotion

c. Applying for new jobs

3. Social

a. Going out twice a week

b. Spending more time with friends

c. Plan a family holiday

If you don't like the idea of manually drawing a mind map, you can use online software to do this. The best mind mapping software available in the market these days is as follows.

- MindMeister
- LucidChart
- Cacoo
- Mindomo
- XMind
- MindManager
- Canava

- Padlet
- Mind Genius
- Mindmap
- Coggle

Chapter Eight: The Power of Vision Boards

What is a Vision Board?

The law of attraction states that your general attitude and beliefs in life tend to act like a magnet that attracts different circumstances, events, and opportunities that allow you to live out all those beliefs and attitudes. The law of attraction is a compelling suggestion that provides an opportunity to shape your life by attracting and manifesting your deepest desires. One of the best ways to leverage the power of the law of attraction is by creating a vision board.

A vision board is more than merely cutting and pasting different magazine cutouts and pictures on a sheet of paper or board. It is a simple tool that helps consciously remind you of your goals and dreams. A vision board is also known as a dream board, and it helps narrow down all your true desires through the power of choice. If you want to vision board to work, then it must clearly show the life you wish to lead. It can include magazine cutouts, images, inspirational quotes, or anything else you want to include. A conventional vision board is made by taking different cutouts of images and texts from magazines or any other printed media onto a corkboard, poster, or a sturdy board of your choice. If you don't like the idea of spending time creating a vision board like this, then you can use various online applications to do the same. You will learn about all these things in this section.

Benefits of a Vision Board

Zero In On a Goal

So, how does a vision board work? The power of choice, visualization, and consistency are the three critical ingredients upon which a vision board's power rests. A vision board forces you to understand and examine all your desires. It enables you to concentrate only on the goals that matter the most to you. This simple process of choosing what you wish to put on the vision board is meaningful. Start by identifying your deepest desires and then selecting images, pictures, and text representing those desires. For instance, if your dream is to purchase a house, then you might place a picture of a house on the vision board. However, if you are unhappy with pasting just one image, you can find various representations of your dreams and make a collage of all the kinds of houses you like and paste it on the vision board.

Makes You Believe

By focusing on the small details, your mind is forced to analyze things that matter the most to you carefully. The power of visualization can never be underestimated. This board's visual aspect is the primary factor that helps drive home the message about your desires. When you start visualizing, concentrate on all the little details associated with your goal. Concentrate on the feelings, emotions, surroundings, external environment, the way your body feels, and everything else you can think of. When you do it right, the act of visualization is almost as powerful as performing the act itself. It helps you focus on the things you desire and then fills you with positive energy and motivation required to keep going.

A vision board helps you realize your dream in your mind, so you believe it is possible to accomplish that dream.

Brings About Consistency

Consistency is essential in life, and it is quintessential for attaining success. Whether or not you are trying to form a new habit, work on your goals, or learn a new skill, you need consistency. The human brain is wired for repetition. Whenever you repeat an action, the said action becomes more robust and more refined. Create a vision board and place it in a place such that you can see it daily. By consistently visualizing your goals, you are training yourself to manifest your deepest desires.

Steps to Follow

Step 1: Start Planning

The first step is to plan the kind of vision board you wish to create. Think about the message your personalized vision board must convey and how you want it to look. You must ask yourself some questions before you can create a vision board, and they are as follows.

What are your goals or desires you want the vision board to reflect?

The different areas of your life you can consider while setting a goal are your values, career, family, love, life, health, and wellness. You can also think about how you would want to spend your free time or think about the life you want to lead.

Do You Want to Create a Single Board or Multiple Boards?

Some like creating small boards for visualizing different categories of their streams, while others prefer making one large board that includes everything they desire. Remember that regardless of the vision board's size, you must place it such that you can look at it daily. So, consider the space available.

What Are the Different Types of Images You Want to Use?

Do you want to print out images? Do you want to use any photographs you have at hand? Do you want to cut out images and pictures from magazines or any other print media? You can also print pictures from your Pinterest board or any quotes from the Internet. Besides this, you can stick pages from a book, flyers, brochures, and pamphlets on the vision board. The sky is the limit with a vision board.

How Do You Want the Vision Board to Look?

Do you want the vision board to look messy or tidy? Some people like their vision board to be crowded and cluttered with different things, while others prefer to look tidy and neat. Once again, it is up to you. You can also add various decorative elements to this board. You can also think about placing certain crystals or even burning some soothing incense near the vision board. Crystals can be charged with your intentions, and they also help manifest the law of attraction. You can use helpful crystals like clear quartz, amethyst, sapphire, rose quartz, tourmaline, citrine, and so on to strengthen your vision board.

Step #2: Gather Supplies

Once you have decided about all the different things you want to include in and around the vision board, it is time to gather all the supplies you require. It might take you a little while to gather all the images, pictures, quotes, or anything else you want to add to the vision board. Remember that you can always keep adding onto the vision board. You need not make it perfect on the first attempt. You can also write quotes on the vision board that inspire you.

Step #3: Get Started

Now that you have everything ready, it is time to get started. While creating a vision board, find a quiet spot for yourself. You can also play some calming and soothing music in the background while burning from incidents. All these things help calm your mind and enable you to think about your dreams and goals. Before you start, you can meditate for a while or send out a silent prayer to the universe to help you. You are seeking the energy of the universe to help you here. So, sending out a prayer might be helpful.

Step #4: Using the Vision Board

The vision board can express a literal, complicated, or metaphorical story. As long as it is the accurate representation of your deepest desires, the story can be expressed in any way. Ensure that everything you put on the vision board mirrors your goals and aspirations of life. So, whenever you look at this board, thoughts about your goals and aspirations must immediately come to your mind. Once you have created the vision board, it is time to use it. Don't forget to place this vision board at your home such that you see it every day. You can place it on your nightstand or any other place you want. Place it such this vision board is the first thing you look at as soon as you wake up in the morning and the last thing before you go to sleep at night. Make it a point to set for about 10 minutes with your vision board at least once or twice a week. Visualize all the goals you want to achieve in life. This visualization will give you the motivation and energy you require to keep going.

Digital Vision Boards

If you like arts and crafts or DIY projects, you can make the vision board at home. It hardly takes an hour or two to make the vision board. However, if you are running short of time or don't like indulging in DIY projects, you can always choose a digital version. You can create a digital vision board using online software or applications. A great thing about a digital vision board is that you can easily access it anywhere since you can carry its softcopy with you.

Most of the online software or applications offer a massive database of inspiring photographs, quotes, and themes you can use to set up the vision board. You don't have to sit and collect these supplies; merely use the resources available online. The different vision board applications and websites to turn your dreams into reality are as follows.

- DreamItAlive
- Visuapp
- Corkulous Professional
- iWish
- MindMovies
- Canva
- Hay House Vision Board

Chapter Nine: Goals and Time Management

Managing your time wisely is probably the most powerful skill that can take you places in life. Time management helps you in different life stages and isn't just confined to your professional life. If you are not using your time wisely, the chances are slim that you will ever reach your goals or even get anything done. One thing that is constant for everyone regardless of their age, sex, geographical location, or any other demographic factor is how time passes by: time doesn't wait for anyone, and if you keep squandering this precious resource away, you will never get to your destination. We all have precisely 24-hours or 86,400 seconds in a day. Regardless of what you might want to or wish to believe, this is all the time you must work with. The way you organize your daily schedule and utilize your time matters a lot when it comes to attaining your goals.

So, what is time management? Time management is a simple process of planning and organizing how you divide all the time available to you daily for different activities. Time management ensures that you are not only working harder but smarter too. It helps you accomplish more in less time. Time management improves your overall efficiency and productivity, helps build your reputation, reduces stress, opens up different opportunities, and helps you succeed in life. Remember that being busy differs from being productive. Unless you are productive and engage in activities that bring you a step closer to your goal, you are merely wasting your time.

The inability to effectively prioritize, procrastination, and unrequited laziness are among the leading factors for improper time management. Regardless of the goals you have set for yourself, you cannot attain them if you don't learn to manage your time effectively. In this section, let us look at some simple tips you can follow to attain your goals using time management.

Tip #1: Existing Routine

To become better at managing your time, then you must become aware of your current routine. Spend some time and think about the way you spend your time daily. You can maintain a journal. However, these days there are plenty of task reminders and to-do list apps you can use to track the time spent. Think about the last ten days and notice how you spend your time. You can immediately identify patterns. For instance, you might realize that your productivity is high in the morning while it reduces around the evening. So, you can schedule the most important tasks early in the morning and reduce your burden toward the evening. By optimizing the time available and concentrating on essential tasks, you can accomplish more.

Tip #2: Start Prioritizing

To be successful, and wish to accomplish your goals in life, then you must start prioritizing. We all have plenty of things that take away our attention. So, unless you concentrate on the things that matter, you get nothing done. The best way to prioritize your tasks is by completing the most critical and daunting tasks before moving onto anything else.

Here is a sample of the time management matrix. In this matrix, you must divide a paper into four parts. Each quadrant represents a specific task or set of tasks. The four quadrants are as follows.

Tasks that are important and urgent: All these tasks are important and require your immediate attention. They have a high urgency rate and must be completed within a deadline. Get to these tasks right away.

Tasks that are important but not urgent: All these tasks are important, but they are not urgent. So, you can put them on hold for a while. They don't need your immediate attention, but it doesn't mean you forget about them. To improve your ability to manage your time, then concentrate on all the tasks that fall under this category.

Tasks that are not important but are urgent: There will be specific tasks that are quite urgent but are not necessary. You can easily delegate, minimize, or even eliminate these tasks since they don't contribute toward any of your goals.

Tasks that are not important and not urgent: These tasks offer little or no value altogether. They don't help you attain your goals. These tasks merely drain out your time and energy. Whenever you place specific tasks in this category, it is time to eliminate them. Try eliminating these tasks as much as you can to do more things.

Tip #3: Understand Your Goals

Ensure that the goal you have set is the right one for you. This step has been mentioned several times until now because it is quite vital. If the goal you set is not the right one for you, then you can never succeed. Instead of setting yourself up for disappointment, it is time to rewire the way you think. Understand your goals and your reasons for attaining them. Whenever in doubt, revisit the steps and tips discussed in previous chapters to understand your goals better.

Tip #4: Time Limits

A simple way to ensure that you make most of the 24 hours available at your disposal is by setting time limits for all the tasks you engage in throughout the day. Reading and replying to emails can be time-consuming. However, it must not be the only task you complete within the 24 hours available. When you assign specific time limits for specific tasks, you can manage your time instead of allowing the tasks to guide your daily routine. For instance, if you have set an hour aside to read and respond to emails, then do things within that hour. If it exceeds the time limit, then move on to the next task. Once you have completed all the other tasks you planned, you can go back to any task left unfinished. By doing this, you can ensure that you are completing all your tasks wasting no time.

Tip #5: Planning Ahead

In the previous steps, you were shown how you could prioritize different tasks at hand. Once you know your priorities, it is time to start planning. Spend some time and think about all the activities you must complete and how you want to complete them. It takes up a little time, but it is time well spent. You can make a to-do list, set a plan of action, or even set specific goals for the days to come. Usually, we all get caught up in mundane activities and daunting tasks we forget about planning. If you are unsure how to plan duties, you can do this either early in the morning or before you go to bed.

Before you sleep at night, spend some time and take a couple of minutes to clear your head. Once you feel calm, make a list of all the tasks you want to accomplish on the following day. When the list is ready, prioritize them in the order of their importance. So, as soon as you wake up in the morning, you will have an idea of all the important tasks you must complete before attending to anything else. It helps improve your overall productivity while giving you a better sense of purpose. Also, you will feel satisfied when you complete all the critical tasks within the given timeframe. If you don't want to do this at night, you can make up in the morning and set a couple of minutes aside to do this before working on anything else.

Tip #6: Walk Away

Keep trying and pushing yourself. However, you must also know when to stop and where to draw the line. It is okay to abandon a sinking ship instead of sinking with it. Walk away from any tasks, projects, or activities you know are headed toward an unfortunate destination. If they are headed nowhere, there is no point in wasting any of your time, energy, effort trying to complete them. It is OK to move on from an unproductive task toward something more productive. It is acceptable to know where you must spend your energy. If a specific task doesn't turn out the way you thought it would. Even after making all the possible effort, stop beating yourself up. Instead, realize that the time you have invested has passed you by. Learn the lesson; life is trying to teach you, and move on. , you can probably avoid making the mistakes you made in the past.

Tip #7: Say No

You are the only one who can decide what is right for you. If something doesn't feel right, or if you do want to do something, you can say no. Don't be under any misconceptions that you'll come across as being selfish if you say no. Learning to say no is a skill that comes in handy in all aspects of your life. Learning to say no is also quintessential for time management. Remember, you are the boss, and no one else can tell you otherwise.

If you have an important deadline or something urgent, you must work on it, then prioritize your own work. Don't go out with your friends or help a colleague when you are flooded with work. Do things, and then concentrate on the other things. It is more important to attend to the issues that matter for moving toward your own goals instead of focusing on what others need. Therefore, prioritize your needs and concentrate on getting things done.

Sometimes, you cannot say no. In such instances, delegate work. Once you delegate your responsibilities to someone else, stop thinking about it and don't try to micromanage if you cannot say no, you will never learn how to manage all the time available to you effectively.

Tip #8: Start Decluttering

Decluttering is all about getting rid of clutter. When you work in an environment filled with unnecessary clutter, you lose focus and lose track of the task at hand. It is one reason why you must keep your workspace tidy and organized. When you lose focus, you essentially squander precious time. Take a couple of minutes daily to clean up your workspace. If your workspace is cluttered with old files, office stationery, or things you don't need, remove them. Your desk must be neat, organized, and tidy. Cleaning and decluttering can be relaxing.

Tip #9: Find Balance

To reduce the stress you feel, then it is unquestionably necessary that you balance your personal and professional life. You cannot concentrate only on one aspect of your life to get ahead. To avoid burnout in your daily life, learn to recognize the importance of work-life balance. The absence of this balance increases the stress you feel. Once you feel stressed, it becomes easier to indulge in bad habits, and these bad habits will eventually take away your concentration from your goals. While working, take a couple of breaks sometimes. You cannot concentrate on a specific task for over 45 minutes at a stretch. Once the 45 minutes are up, give yourself a break for five minutes. In this break, you can get yourself a cup of coffee, talk to someone you want, or maybe even just relax. Regardless of what you do, keep giving yourself a few mental breaks.

Tip #10: Get Rid of Distractions

It is not just decluttering that matters, but you must also remove distractions for improving your productivity. Decluttering your physical space is as important as decluttering the mental space available to you too. Our usual habits lean toward distractions and allow our minds to wander for longer than required. All these things merely lead to an additional waste of time. It could be in a colleague interrupting you while working, checking your social media, playing any games, or attending a call while in the meeting. All these things essentially take away your mental ability to concentrate on the task at hand. Also, don't try multitasking.

You might think you can do more things if you're working on various tasks simultaneously. Well, multitasking merely leads to wastage of your precious mental energy. Think of your entire attention span as a bucket. Every task you work on puts a small hole in this bucket. If you are working on several things at once, then multiple holes will form in this bucket, and it can hold no water within. So, get rid of distractions, concentrate on one thing at a task, and move onto the next only after completing the task at hand.

By following the simple tips discussed in this section, you can ensure that you are getting more things accomplished within the given time frame. If you follow these tips for a couple of weeks, you will notice a positive change in the way you spend your time.

Chapter Ten: Focus, Motivation, and Self-Discipline

Stay Focused and Motivated

What is the difference between those who succeed and everyone else? What do successful people do that most of us fail to do? Sure, talent, luck, and hard work matter. There is another critical aspect we all overlook, and it is the ability to keep going even when boredom strikes. We all talk about staying motivated and being passionate. People lose motivation or feel depressed when they believe successful people have unstoppable willpower and passion. They do have willpower and passion, but they also know how to keep going when boredom strikes. There is no magic pill they use to feel inspired and ready to tackle all the challenges. Those who succeed and wish to attain their goals don't allow their emotions to guide their actions. Top performers work through the border and embrace the daily practice and consistency required to attain them. It isn't easy to work when it isn't easy. Anyone can work when feeling pumped up and motivated. However, when this motivation falters, you must still keep going to attain your goals.

We live in a world filled with distractions from unlimited web access to constant messaging; staying focused and constructive can become difficult. In this section, you will learn about simple tips you can follow to stay motivated and focused on your goals.

Money Might Not Be Motivating

Money is important, and it can be a motivating factor. However, money cannot be the only motivating factor. Many people wrongly assume that money will motivate them to keep going. In the initial stages, it can work, but sustaining financial motivation becomes tricky if the work you are doing keeps dragging on. When you work long enough, you will realize money is not worth compromising on different aspects of your life. If the activities associated with your goal are tedious, tiring, or too complicated, then money cannot be a motivating factor. Also, if these activities are not in sync with who you are and what you want to do in life, setting and attaining goals will become tricky.

Are They Your Goals?

Another common obstacle in staying motivated and following through on goals is ensuring that the goals you have set are the ones you genuinely want to attain. At times, we set goals based on what others think or what others feel we should be doing. Instead of concentrating on what we want to do, we give undue importance to what others think. You can always ask others for their opinions but ensure that the goals you set hold some personal value for you. If they represent no personal values, you probably will prematurely give up on them. So, spend some time, follow the tips and steps discussed in the previous chapters to ensure your goals are your own. There is a significant difference between going after something that you want and what others want.

Visualizing the Results

A simple way to concentrate on your goals and keep up your motivation levels is by visualizing the result you wish to attain. Instead of getting bogged down by all the challenges or complexity of the goal, concentrate on how wonderful you will feel when you attain the goals. Visualize the result. How will you feel when you attain your goal? You'll probably feel relieved and incredibly excited. Concentrate on these two feelings to fuel you on days when you don't want to work. Attaining goals takes hard work, and this hard work can make you want to procrastinate. So, by reminding yourself of what you can achieve with your hard work, you can propel yourself toward attaining the desired results.

Breaking Down the Goals

When you look at a big goal, it can become quickly overwhelming. When it becomes overwhelming, you'll get scared about it, and the initial motivation associated with the goal will fade away. To avoid all this, it is better to break down the goals into simpler and manageable tasks. For instance, if your goal is to reorganize your closet, you can break it down into simpler tasks like reorganizing your shoes, winter clothing, bags, and so on. So, you will be a step closer to attaining your overall goal whenever you complete one simple task. Also, upon completion, you will feel a little satisfied with yourself and motivated to keep going.

Company Matters

The kind of company you maintain matters a lot when it comes to your overall attitude in life. If you surround yourself with people who give out positive energy, you will feel better about yourself. Engage in stimulating conversations about your passions with your close circle. If someone seems unsupportive of your goals, it is time to maintain some distance. Others need not agree with what you say, but you need no negative energy toward your goals. If naysayers surround you, you probably will quickly give up on the goals because you feel you do nothing. Instead, surround yourself with motivated, inspirational, and positive individuals. Their positivity will trickle into your life.

Start Organizing

Start decluttering your thoughts and organize them. Whenever you work on a big goal, a cluttered and overstimulated mind will sap you of all your energy. Instead of allowing yourself to get overwhelmed and drained out like this, it is better to declutter your mind. Sit down for a while and pay attention to all the different thoughts you have about your goals. You can note these thoughts in a journal, or you can talk to your loved ones about them. Once you have a list in place, dedicate a specific time for completing each task. It helps you get what you want without getting sidetracked or overwhelmed.

Concentrate On the Big Picture

Regardless of what you do, ensure that your main goal always stays in your mind. Even while dealing with unpleasant or menial tasks associated with the goal, don't lose sight of it. If you are running low on motivation, remind yourself that your goal is not just about completing a task but also about something much bigger than all this.

Letting Go

There are several factors in your life you cannot control. Instead of worrying about all the external factors you cannot control, it is better to concentrate on controlling and regulating factors. If you keep worrying about things you cannot do, you will feel paralyzed and stuck worrying about the future. Replace all the thoughts that start with "what if" to "I can." Don't contemplate the future. Since you cannot control it. However, you can certainly take action in the present to ensure that you create the kind of future you want.

Be Consistent

Ensure that you are consistent while working toward your goals. Every day make it a point to do at least one thing that puts you a step closer to your goal. It need not be anything significant. For instance, if weight loss is your goal, then make it a point you exercise for at least 30 minutes daily. On days you don't feel like exercising, make sure you are eating healthy and wholesome meals. If not, concentrate on something else you can do to stay on track and attain your goals. Unless you are consistent, your motivational levels are bound to falter.

Follow the simple tips discussed in this section to keep up your motivation levels while going after your life goals.

Developing Self-Discipline

To attain a goal, you need self-discipline. Self-discipline is the force that enables you to move forward and keep going even when you don't feel like doing it. You can keep performing, fulfilling your promises, and meeting all the deadlines essential for becoming successful. Without self-discipline, the momentum required to make progress will be absent. Self-discipline is your ability to regulate and work toward improvement. You can regulate your desires, feelings, and actions.

Self-discipline is about consistently taking small actions that gradually help develop good habits that propel you toward your goals. By integrating these habits into your daily life, it becomes easier to create a lifestyle in sync with your goals. It helps condition and rewires your mind to recognize the long-term rewards associated with every step you take while forgoing behaviors that might cause short-term pleasure. A disciplined mind not only sees but also realizes the importance of waking up early and getting a head start on the day instead of hitting the snooze button for some extra sleep.

Self-discipline is quintessential for becoming successful in all aspects of your life. All successful people are incredibly self-discipline. Self-discipline is the source of persistence, dedication, and inspiration required to overcome any obstacles and challenges that come along your way on the route to success. It enables you to realize and access your innate inner strength. It also improves your confidence and problem-solving abilities. Self-discipline helps you see the bigger picture and forces you to take action even when you don't want to.

Well, do you think you are self-disciplined? To be fair, this is one area in which most of us could use some extra help. The good news is that – as with any other habit – you can develop and improve your self-discipline. In this section, let us look at some simple steps you can follow to develop self-discipline.

Step #1: Understand Your Goals

The first step is to envision and define your goals – what they mean to you and how you want to achieve them. There are two questions you must ask yourself to do this.

• What does success mean to you regarding your goal?

• What are the different steps you must take to reach your destination?

Unless you have some clarity about your goals, you cannot develop self-discipline.

Step #2: Personal Values

What are your personal values? What does your goal mean to you? What is the driving force that keeps you going? What is the value you can attain by achieving a goal? You can develop self-discipline once you start creating personal value in all the goals you set. Unless these goals are valuable to you, you will not want to achieve them, or procrastination will creep in. To avoid all this, you must find your inspirations and motivations and continuously remind yourself of the same.

Step #3: Finding a Role Model

Whatever goal you have, you will not be the only person with that goal. Therefore, spend some time trying to look at all the people who accomplished the same goal you are trying to. For instance, if weight loss is your goal, you can look for inspiration by talking to a friend who achieved the same goal as you. By talking to such people, you can come up with a list of specific behaviors that might have empowered them and given them the strength to keep going even in the face of adversities. You can also learn of the different mistakes they made along the way and try avoiding them. Besides this, you will also learn about all the possible challenges you might face while working toward attaining your goals.

Step #4: What Are The Challenges?

Working toward a goal is seldom easy. So, be prepared to run into particular challenges and obstacles along the way. It would be foolish to expect smooth sailing throughout the journey. All the obstacles you face will challenge your resolve and might even make you question yourself. Once you know the different challenges you might face, you can avoid or overcome them. For instance, if weight loss is your goal, then one obstacle you might face is dealing with the urge to binge on unhealthy foods. So, what can you do? You can come up with healthier alternatives to your favorite snacks or maybe devise an alternate plan to overcome the temptation.

Step #5: Changes

You don't have to change your entire personality to attain a goal. However, there are certain habits or behaviors you can develop to increase your chances of success. Think about your goal, and then make a list of different qualities and skills you need to attain that goal. To do this, you can once again look at successful people and their stories and list their traits and characteristics. Compare yourself with such people, and you will realize the different habits you must develop.

Step #6: Environment Matters

Unless your environment is conducive to growth, you will struggle with self-discipline even if you are in the right state of mind. Your usual environment must support your goals and the habits you must form to attain those goals. For instance, you cannot stay focused on a specific task if you work in a noisy environment. So, you must work on creating an environment that supports your goals and growth.

Step #7: Make a Commitment

Consider all the factors mentioned up until now. Now, it is time to create a detailed plan of action that enables you to make progress. What are the different actions you can take daily? How will you deal with obstacles? What are the changes you must make? Prioritize all the tasks, create milestones, and set certain rewards that enable you to move toward your goals.

Step #8: Tracking Your Progress

A simple way to stay focused, motivated, and disciplined is by turning your progress. Maintain a journal that enables you to see the progress you make and areas where there is scope for improvement. Note all things working for you and that make you feel good. Also, don't forget to include details about things that don't work for you. Periodically look at the journal entries, make adjustments as required, and it will help you stay focused.

Step #9: Understand Your Emotions

Most of us allow our emotions to regulate us instead of regulating our emotions. Therefore, learn to identify and interpret your emotions so you can effectively deal with various situations in life. If things don't feel as they are supposed to, or like you're expected, explore other approaches. Don't allow your emotions to guide your decisions.

Step #10: Inspiration

Maintaining self-discipline becomes a little complicated when dealing with adversity. It is where inspiration steps into the picture. You can explore different sources of inspiration like mindfulness, meditation, reading books, talking to your mentors, watching inspirational movies, and so on. It is easy to keep going when you feel inspired.

Follow these ten simple steps to develop self-discipline. Don't expect any miraculous changes overnight. It takes some time and effort to form a new habit. So, be patient and commit yourself.

Chapter Eleven: Goal Reviewing and Reflection

Benefits of Goal Reviewing and Reflection

Your work doesn't end once you set goals. You need to continuously and consistently work toward attaining those goals. Along the way, you must also review and reflect upon all these goals and the progress you make. Regardless of the goal you set, by reviewing your goals consistently, you can produce consistent results. When you lose sight of your goals, it might make you feel like you are fighting an uphill battle, and it can harm your inclination to keep going. So, let us look at the different benefits of reviewing and reflecting on the goals you set.

An essential benefit of establishing a goal is that it enables you to determine the course of action you must take to reach your desired destination. By reviewing your plan of action or the quintessential roadmap daily, you'll be better equipped to execute any plan you come up with. When you keep reminding yourself of the different steps you must take, it will come to you automatically. Then, reaching your target or goal becomes an inevitable destination.

Without all this, you merely end up with a destination with no roadmap of reaching it.

Your goals will be forgotten if you don't keep repeating them. You might have probably listened to a song that got stuck in your mind, and you kept replaying it in your mind later. However, this memory will only last for a couple of days. If you stop listening to the song, you will quickly forget the lyrics. Likewise, you must frequently review your goals to ensure that you can recall the steps you must take to attain them. Besides that, it also enables you to understand the different benchmarks for reviewing the goals. The more you do this, the probability of implementing the desired actions increases. When you frequently review the steps, it eventually creates a new neural pathway in your mind to not forget about your goals. When your goals stay in your memory, every action you take consciously or unconsciously goes back to the goal you want to achieve.

When you review your goals, it adds to the daily motivation you feel. Make it a point to review your goals when you wake up and once before you go to sleep. In the morning, remind yourself of your purpose and all that you wish to accomplish. Before you go to sleep, reflect on the day you had and all the highlights. If you feel there is some scope for improvement, don't forget to make the required changes. For instance, if you realized that you spent more time answering emails than you were supposed to, you can think about automating certain emails' responses.

If you don't review your goals, you will eventually lose the desire to attain them. When you lose this vital desire, the goal loses its value along the way. If there is no sense of urgency, desire often loses its value. Goals will also eventually lose value when you don't review them. Ensure that you review your goals once every day to avoid any mindless action. When you keep thinking about your goals, your thoughts become actions. Once you take action, you can attain your goals.

You cannot achieve a goal overnight, and it takes consistent hard work and effort. So, whenever you make some progress, don't forget to review it. When you see that you are making progress, it not only makes you feel happy, but it gives you a sense of accomplishment that enables you to work toward your goals. When your personal value increases, your self-worth increases. Even if the progress isn't significant, the knowledge you made some progress will keep you going.

Steps to Follow

Now that you're aware of the different benefits review and reflection offers, it is time to incorporate certain simple practices into your daily routine. Here are a couple of different tips you can follow.

Relevancy of the Goal

Every goal you establish is based on your existing situation in life. Since life doesn't exist in a vacuum, change is inevitable. When your life changes, you must review your goals to ensure they are still relevant. For instance, if your goal was to get a promotion, but you changed jobs before accomplishing the goal, it is time to review and tweak the goal to meet your new requirements. If the goal loses its relevance, then you will have no desire to achieve it. So, ask yourself whether your situation has changed significantly? If there have been any significant changes, is the goal still relevant? Are you still keen on attaining your goals? Is this what you want to do? Remember, unless the goal is irrelevant, you will not have the motivation to attain them. Remind yourself why you set the goal in the first place, and introspect whether the reasons hold true for you in the present scenario.

Measuring Your Progress

Regardless of the goal you set, you must be able to track and measure the progress. You can use a ranking system or even an actual measure like weight to measure any progress you make. For instance, if your goal is to lose 20 pounds within six months, then a simple measure you can use is your bodyweight. If you notice any changes in your body weight in a positive direction, it means you are successfully working toward your goals. Likewise, if you notice you are gaining weight, it means you might need to change your diet or exercise routine to get back on track. To measure any progress you make, go back to your starting point and compare it with your situation. If you notice an upward swing, it means you are closer to attaining your goals than you were earlier. If you think you're not on track, it is time for a little self-introspection. It is where reflection comes into the picture. Reflect upon all that you did and the reasons you went off track. With a little self-reflection, you can quickly identify the different obstacles that pushed you off course. By taking corrective action to overcome these obstacles, you can quickly get back on track.

Action Plan

Your goal is the end destination, whereas your action plan is the roadmap you can use to reach the destination. If you don't use this plan, then how can you ever reach your destination? Take some time and think about your plan of action and any other alternate options available. Don't worry if you need to make specific changes to your goals. Change is an inevitable part of life, and you cannot shy away from it. Therefore, adapt yourself to the change, and try to reframe your goals to stay relevant and suit your needs.

If you set any deadline for yourself, it is time to review whether you have met those deadlines. If you fail to meet deadlines, there is a reason for it. Deadlines are established since it helps build momentum. Maybe the deadlines were unrealistic, or perhaps other urgent activities needed your immediate attention. Reflect upon why you missed the deadlines. If your deadlines were impractical, then come up with something more practical. Regardless of your plan of action, ensure that you allow a little wiggle room for yourself. Life is unpredictable, and things can change in the blink of an eye. Therefore, try to make some room to accommodate all these unpredictable changes.

If you think your timeframe and the action plan are both ideal, then stick to it. However, in your review, if you notice you couldn't, then understand the reasons for the same.

Resources

Do you have sufficient resources to support your goals? It could be in the form of time, support, information, or even finances. Is anything preventing you from attaining your goals? Do you think you are honestly struggling to attain the goal? Regardless of what it is, never spread yourself out too thin. If you do this, you will eventually burn yourself out and increase the stress you experience. To prevent all this, you might need to readjust your plan of action. Maybe you need a while longer than you thought. If that's the case, then it is okay to alter your deadlines. However, ensure that the deadlines are realistic and don't place your goals on the backburner for too long. If you do this, any momentum you gained until this point will soon dispel. If you are running short of resources, then maybe it is time to consider how you can increase your resources.

Review

How did you prepare and plan for a specific goal you want to attain? While reviewing, was there anything in the review that set your alarm bells off? Do you think you're still on track to attaining your goals? Do you still have sight of the big picture? Is there something holding you back? Are there any bad habits or weaknesses preventing you from attaining your goals? Can you draw on any of your strengths to help yourself? Carefully consider all these questions while you review the progress you make. Here are a couple of other questions you can ask yourself during the review and reflection session.

- What are the different things you are doing that are enabling you to work toward your goal? (Well, keep doing these things and keep up your excellent work!)

- Are you happy with the progress you are making? (If yes, then you are on the right track. If not, you must make changes to your plan of action to increase your progress.)

- Is the goal more manageable than you thought it would be?

- Is the goal harder than you initially believed? (If yes, then you need to work on improving your motivation levels to attain the goal. you can use a vision board.)

- Do you think you need to take small steps?

- Do you think you need to take more significant steps, and will you be able to do this?

- How can you improve yourself to attain your goals?

- Are you excited about the goal? Do you like working on your goal? (If yes, then it means you chose the right goal. if not, it is time to review your goal and perhaps replace it with something you enjoy.)

- Are you sticking to your core values while you work toward your goals? (Go back and review your core values. If you are diverting from them, then maybe you need to replace your goal. If you compromise on your core values, it can cause unnecessary internal conflict, preventing you from working on your goals.)

Reflection (Success/Failure Analysis)

Once you work toward your goals, you will find a couple of victories, and for some failures. Success and failure are two sides of the same coin. One cannot exist without the other. So, you must maintain a positive attitude, regardless of the outcome. Never give up on your goal because you might encounter an obstacle or experience failure. True failure is when you stop working on your goal and believe it is the end of the road. It is all about your mindset. Whenever you feel, don't give up. Instead, use this precious opportunity to analyze all the things that went wrong. It enables you to gather knowledge that will improve any goal-setting process you undertake.

Concentrate on the failures, but don't forget about all the victories that come your way. Don't get so overwhelmed thinking or worrying about failure that you forget to celebrate your success. Analyze all the events that led to your success. It will enable you to realize the things that contribute to the achievement of your goals. Once you realize these things, you can spend more of your time and energy engaging in such practices that are desirable. It enables you to understand what works for you. You must keep reviewing your goals as you work toward attaining them. It's not just review, but you must also reflect on the outcomes.

This review identifies all the things you did well and the ones you didn't. Most important, it enables you to understand how you can improve or the things you can do differently in the future to meet your goals.

Check-Ins

A short-term goal is something that you wish to attain within a month. For such goals, you must review them at least once every week. You don't have to review it daily, but try to do it on every alternate day. A quarterly goal is a goal you wish to accomplish within three months. Ensure that you review it every week to ensure you are on the right track. A semi-annual goal is something you want to achieve within six months. You must review it at least once a month. If you think it is essential, you can review it once a week. An annual goal is something you wish to accomplish within a year. You must review it twice every year and can include it in your quarterly review. If you have any long-term goals (five years or longer), don't forget to review them twice every year.

While reviewing these goals, ensure that you don't lose focus on the smaller goals you set. Every goal is equally important. If you get overwhelmed by setting multiple goals, then stick to one or, at the most, five goals and work on them consistently.

If you are maintaining a journal or an app to check your progress, ensure there is a sufficient place to add notes as time goes by. You might need to slightly modify individual goals or make notes when you cannot achieve a specific goal. Regardless of the outcome, don't give up on the goal and keep up your hard work.

Chapter Twelve: Obstacles and Mistakes in Goal Setting

Common Obstacles to Goal Setting

There are a couple of common obstacles you must avoid while setting goals. These obstacles can make all the difference between success and failure for attaining your goals. So, let us look at them and how to avoid them in this section.

Too Many Commitments

We all have plenty of things we have to accomplish daily. It is not just your daily chores, but you must also concentrate on the goals you want to attain. So, how can you squeeze in more things while concentrating on your goals? The simplest way to make the most of the time available to you while concentrating on your set goals is by eliminating, automating, and delegating certain tasks. All the things you considered neither essential nor urgent must be eliminated from your daily agenda. Try automating your daily chores. You can automate your bill payments and email responses. Every minute you save is an additional minute to concentrate on your goals. If you know someone else can do the same task efficiently, then delegate. When you delegate, you can concentrate only on the things that matter and require your attention.

Stressing Out

Stop stressing out. You cannot accomplish your goals if you keep stressing out about them. External factors can cause stress, but eventually, it all boils down to how you deal with it. The workload does not stress you out; it is the way you carry it. That adds to the stress. So, it is time to work on reducing and regulating your stress levels. Stress is not just tiring mentally, but it can also harm your physical wellbeing. You can try meditation, take regular breaks while working, and add some exercise to your daily routine. You don't have to exercise or meditate for hours on end. Set about 20 to 30 minutes aside daily for de-stressing. Once your mind is free from stress, it becomes easier to concentrate on your goals. Also, it gives you the mental energy required to review and reflect on the goals you have set for yourself.

Time Constraints

Time is an essential and limited resource. You can feel rather frustrated when you have too many things to accomplish within a short period. We all have a fixed number of hours available at our disposal. So, making the most of it is quintessential for attaining a goal. Ensure that you have a good morning routine. Wake up early in the morning and concentrate on the most critical tasks of the day. When you get these important tasks out of the way, it becomes easier to allocate the available time toward all the other tasks. Also, make it a point not to stay up late at night. Use the different tips about time management in the previous section to develop a daily schedule for yourself.

Ensure that you get at least 6 to 7 hours of good quality and undisturbed sleep every night. Your body and mind need sufficient rest if you want them to keep performing optimally. Remember the age-old saying, "The early bird catches the worm?" It will do you good to remember this when it comes to time management.

Don't Try to be a Perfectionist

We all desire perfection, but if you get obsessed with perfection, you will get nothing done. No plan will ever be perfect, and you will keep second-guessing every decision you make until it reaches your desired level of perfection. To attain your goals, ensure that you are *taking action* instead of just planning out every detail. At times, the best course of action is to take the first step instead of thinking about it. Use the 80% approach to lose the perfectionist attitude and overcome procrastination. It essentially says that you must invent, execute, or take some action, but not do it to its fullest. You will only complete about 80% of the task. This increases your confidence and builds momentum. The 80% must include the trickiest tasks you must undertake to attain your goal. When this significant chunk is out of the way, you will be left with 20% of the easy work. You might even delegate the rest to someone else.

Lack of Energy

Sometimes, you think, "I have no energy to do anything else." After a tiring day, you might not want to work on your goals. There will be days when life can easily overwhelm you or get in the way. You must plan your days wisely and use your energy optimally. Your overall energy is like a freshly baked pie. Whenever you add an activity to your daily routine, one slice of this pie is removed. So, carefully consider whether the tasks you partake in daily add value to your life or not.

So, ensure that you take good care of yourself. Self-care is your responsibility, and there is no way in which you can delegate it to others. You cannot do away with self-care. Unless you care for your body, mind, and soul, they will not serve you optimally. It is not just about planning your days, but you must be considerate of your energy at your disposal if you try to do too many things at once, the potential of a burnout increases. When this happens, any motivation you had toward attaining the goal will quickly fade away.

Losing Your Drive

Losing your motivation or the desire to keep going is one obstacle you must never overlook. During the initial stage, you might hit the ground running, make some good progress, and then suddenly, you no longer have the drive to keep going. The road to success is never straightforward, and it keeps meandering in unexpected ways. Whenever your motivation tank is running dangerously low, it is time to remind yourself of the reasons you want to attain your goal. You must thoroughly understand your goal and your reasons for wanting to achieve that goal. Unless you understand all this, you will eventually lose the motivation to keep going. You can use the different tips about motivation in the previous chapters to ensure that you don't lose your drive.

Goal-Setting Mistakes to Avoid

Goals can inspire and motivate you to become successful. They give you a clear sense of direction and enable you to effectively prioritize the different tasks you must complete. When you make certain mistakes while setting goals, these goals become a burden and will hinder you instead of inspiring you. Setting goals might seem like a piece of cake. However, unless you do it right, your chances of success are low. Unless you set practical goals, you cannot make the right decisions. Unless you make the right decisions, your overall productivity will suffer. Poor decisions are directly proportional to poor results. So, to turn your life around, then you must set practical goals for yourself.

Mistakes are life's way of teaching you important lessons. However, it doesn't mean you must keep making mistakes to learn. You can learn a lot from the mistakes that others make. In this section, let us look at some common goal-setting mistakes and how you can avoid them.

Tasks vs. Goals

A common mistake many people make while setting goals is that they set tasks instead of goals. A practical goal helps challenge you and unlock your potential. The goals must be challenging so you can grow as a person while working on attaining them. If the goal you set can be achieved with no growth, then you have not established a goal for yourself. Instead, you merely set up a couple of tasks you must complete.

Internal Conflict

It has been mentioned time and again in this book: the goal you set must never directly conflict with your identity or purpose. The goals must be consistent with the kind of person you are, want to be, and your values. Unless they serve you, you cannot work on attaining them. For instance, if honesty is one of your core values, then the goals you set must not encourage dishonest behavior. If there is any conflict of interest, it causes severe internal dilemmas that can demotivate you instead of inspiring you.

For Others

Ensure that the goal you set is only for yourself and not for others. Well, if your goals are based on any expectations that others will change, you are setting yourself up for disappointment. Set goals only for yourself. You cannot control the way others are, regardless of how hard you wish it otherwise. The only thing you can control is your life and your reactions. If you set goals for others, you have no control over the goals. Also, you have no right to determine how the other person is supposed to live their lives. You can state your opinions and preferences, but you cannot dictate terms about how others must live. For instance, your goal might be to lead a healthier life. To do this, you might have stopped drinking alcohol. Merely because you did this, it doesn't mean others have to follow. You can encourage them to do this, but you cannot force them.

Out of Your Control

You cannot set goals for things beyond your purview of control. The only thing you can control is your thoughts and actions. These are the two things you can always control. If your goals depend on others or on things you cannot control, you are setting yourself up for failure and disappointment. For instance, a goal like "I will get promoted if my boss changes," is not something you can control.

Too Generic

Your goals cannot inspire or motivate you if they aren't detailed. If your goals are vague and generic, your desire to follow suit will reduce. A generic goal might be to lead a happy life, become healthy and fit, or earn more money. These goals explain a generic state of being and not the specific steps you must take to attain them. If you aren't aware of the steps you must take, you can never reach your destination. Therefore, the goals must be detail-oriented. For instance, "I want to lose weight" is a generic goal. An explicit goal is, "I want to lose 20 pounds within six months." When the goal is detailed, it becomes easier to flesh out a plan of action for attaining it.

What You Don't Want

We all know the things we don't like or don't desire. For instance, you might not want to be unhappy, unhealthy, and so on. These are not goals; they are personal statements about your dislikes. Your goal must concentrate on the things you want and desire in life. They should be related to your vision, mission, and core values. Unless a goal is in sync with all this, it cannot be attained. You must know the action you must take to attain the goals. So, start concentering on the positive aspects of a goal instead of concentrating on the things you don't desire.

Looking for Perfection

If you desire perfection in everything you do, you are setting yourself up for disappointment. Remember that you are a human, and you are bound to make a couple of poor decisions and mistakes. If you have a perfectionist attitude in mind, these mistakes will seem like a failure. If you desire absolute perfection from your goal, you are setting yourself up for unnecessary disappointment and failure. Instead, ensure that you are realistic about your goals. Regardless of the time taken, the goal you set must be realistic. It doesn't mean you must not dream big. You can, but ensure that you can also attain them through hard work.

Setting mistakes while establishing goals can seriously harm any progress you make. At times, it can also be the source of incredible stress while you push yourself to achieve goals in direct conflict with your beliefs or values. Goal setting is powerful and will motivate you, provided you do it properly. Go through the different mistakes in this section and tips to avoid them while setting new goals.

Chapter Thirteen: Goal Achieved – Now What?

Take a moment and rejoice in your victory. You have attained your goal! It has been quite a journey, and you have successfully reached your destination. So, what can you do now that you have attained your goals? After you pat yourself on the back for making it this far, it is time to keep practicing good habits daily. All the changes you made to your life and mindset while working toward your goals must stay with you. You cannot forget about them or stop practicing them after you attain your goal. Goal setting is a lifelong process. You can take a break in the middle, but you can never stop if you want to be successful. All the different tips you learned about setting goals, focus, motivation, and productivity must be implemented every day. Becoming self-disciplined is a valuable trait you must never let go of. So, what now? It is time to keep up your motivation levels while developing certain desirable habits that will enable you to stay successful in life.

In this section, you'll learn about simple steps you can follow to develop daily habits for maintaining your overall sense of motivation and self-discipline.

Developing Daily Habits

Decide

You cannot develop a good habit unless you make a conscious decision to do so. To be more self-discipline, it must be a conscious decision. So, it is time to decide what you want to start or stop doing. If you're used to procrastination, then a good habit is to avoid procrastination and instill self-discipline. You must be sure of the way and time at which you wish to incorporate the new behavior. For instance, if your goal is to wake up early every day to concentrate on your goals, you must fix a specific time for that exercise. You cannot just state, "I want to wake up early," instead, it must be something like, "I want to wake up at 6:30 am daily." So, whenever the alarm goes off in the morning, you will know it is time to get out of bed and work on your goals. While deciding this, ensure that the timing is something that you can work with consistently. For instance, if you know that you will be pulling a couple of all-nighters in the next ten days, then waking up at 6:30 A.M. is not realistic.

To incorporate a habit, ensure that it is something you can do daily regardless of the circumstances. If you are confident that it isn't something you'll do consistently, you are merely setting yourself up for disappointment.

Talk to Others

If you are trying to develop a new habit, then talk to your loved ones about the same. Explain the different reasons you want to develop a new habit. It enables you to become more determined and disciplined while you go about learning the new habit. When you know that others expect something specific from you, it puts a little pressure and creates added responsibility. When you know you are accountable to others, your motivation to follow through on your promise also increases. So, discuss your goals with your loved ones. There will be days when you run a little low on motivation. In such instances, your support system can step in and give you the motivation they require to keep going.

No Exceptions

To develop a new habit, there are no exceptions to this rule. Stick to the habit of the routine you wish to inculcate, especially during the formative stages. Now is the time to be a little hard on yourself and don't allow yourself off the hook easily. You are responsible for yourself, and you are accountable for the same. If you wish to develop a new habit, then accountability is quintessential, and no one else can do it for you. Keep a check on yourself, and don't give in to any orders that will deviate you from the new habit you wish to incorporate. You can quickly come up with excuses for rationalizing something you were not supposed to do. For instance, if your goal is to wake up at 6:30 am daily, you must wake up at 6:30 am with no excuses. The only reason you're trying to incorporate a new habit is your improvement. So, it means making a little extra effort during the initial stages. Once you get the hang of it, you will realize that your efforts were truly worth it.

Visualization

A great way to develop a new habit is by visualizing the habit. Think about how wonderful you will feel when you behave in a specific manner. The more time you spend visualizing yourself acting as if you have acquired the habit, the easier it will be to incorporate the same. While visualizing, ensure that your visualization is detailed. For instance, if the new habit you wish to develop is to be more confident, then visualize how wonderful you would feel when you are as confident as you want. Also, by doing this, you are automatically prompting your mind to enable you to act and behave more confidently. Visualization and self-programming go hand-in-hand.

Positive Affirmations

We all tend to have a continuous internal dialogue with ourselves. We think different thoughts, critique our behavior, we praise our effort, and so on. All this is known as your internal talk or self-talk. When this self-talk is predominantly negative, you cannot feel better about yourself. So, pay attention to your self-talk. Ensure that your conversations with yourself are more optimistic. You need to pay a little conscious attention to prevent negative thoughts from creeping up. Even if negative thoughts come up, don't give them too much importance. It doesn't mean you must prevent yourself from thinking negative thoughts; it merely means you must learn to replace them with something more positive. A simple way to do this is by using positive affirmations.

Positive affirmations are statements you can keep repeating to rewire your subconscious. For instance, if your inner critic keeps saying, "I cannot do this," then you must replace it with something more positive. Like, "I cannot do this right now, but I will eventually get there." If you are trying to be more confident, then squish all negative thoughts, replace them with something more positive, like "I am confident." By repeating these positive affirmations daily, you instill a sense of positivity into your subconscious. This positivity is bound to reflect in different aspects of your life. Remember that for positive affirmations to work, you must practice them consistently. Make it a daily habit of setting aside 5 to 10 minutes in the morning to indulge in some positive affirmations.

Rewards

An essential aspect of incorporating a new habit is to create a reward system. Whenever you do something desirable, don't forget to reward yourself for it. By creating a positive association between your actions, and the reward, your motivation to keep at it will increase. You need no one else to cheer or motivate you. Motivation comes from within. So, don't forget to treat yourself whenever you do something desirable. If a daily habit you wish to incorporate is to be more confident and assertive, congratulate yourself whenever you say no! It could be something as simple as watching an episode of your favorite series or maybe even buying some nail polish. The rewards can be simple and need not be anything extravagant.

Persistence

To develop a new habit, you must be persistent and consistent in your first. If you stick by a promise for a week and then give up, it makes little sense. It would be a waste of your time and effort. You must keep practicing the behavior until it comes to you automatically. Once this happens, you no longer have to make any conscious effort to do or not do something. You will feel uncomfortable whenever you deviate from the habit you worked hard to form. Remember that your brain needs consistency in developing new habits. So, learn to be persistent and don't give up.

Make the Habits Stick

It is not just about developing a habit, but you must ensure that the habit you develop *sticks*. If you follow a habit for a couple of weeks and then forget about it, it is counterintuitive to the entire purpose of learning a habit. In this section, let us look at specific simple tips to ensure that any habit you've developed sticks.

To make a habit stick, you must be consistent. If you aim to exercise regularly, ensure that you exercise every day for at least one month. If you exercise once or twice a week, it will become difficult to form a new habit. Consistency is quintessential for developing a new habit. You cannot form a habit if you do things occasionally and not consistently.

To make a habit stick, commit yourself to it for at least 30 days. Bring out your calendar; count the days until the time is up. After the first 30 days, the habit will come to you naturally with no conscious decisions.

Always start simple. If you attempt to do everything at once, you get nothing done. You cannot make a massive overhaul in one day. You cannot change your life in a day. Therefore, learn to be patient with yourself. If you aim to read more daily, then instead of trying to read an entire book on a day, you can start by reading 20 pages daily. After a while, you'll get the hang of it, and you can read for longer. If the habit you try to incorporate clashes with your usual schedule, then the chances of incorporating it into your daily routine decrease.

It would help if you created a trigger to remind yourself of the habit you wish to develop. This trigger can be a ritual or a cue you can follow before executing a habit. For instance, if your idea is to exercise regularly, then a trigger could be drinking a protein shake in the evening before exercising. Whenever you are drinking the protein shake, it is a silent reminder to your mind about the habit you want to develop.

Stop expecting perfection from yourself. It is okay to strive for perfection, but expecting perfection all the time is a recipe for disaster. You can be a little hard on yourself, especially when you don't stick to your habit during an initial couple of days. However, don't be critical to the extent that it dominates any motivation you have. Be patient and compassionate toward yourself. What might work for others doesn't necessarily have to work for you. So, a routine that seems to have worked for a friend might not work for you. If that's the case, don't be disappointed, and merely think of different ways to attain your goals.

Tips for Daily Motivation

Learning to motivate yourself is an important life skill. Motivation isn't random – even if it feels like it is at times. Once you understand how motivation works, it becomes easier to stop procrastination and overcome any inner resistance toward working on your goals. Also, motivation makes your life easier and enjoyable. Since you no longer have to force yourself to do something but experience an inherent desire to do it, life gets easier. For instance, when you feel like doing something, the chances of getting things done high. Likewise, when you don't feel like doing something, you need the motivation to keep going.

Many people wrongly believed that motivation doesn't last. Well, do you brush your teeth daily? Why do you do this? You do it to keep your teeth healthy and clean. Likewise, learning to motivate yourself is not a one-time thing. It is something you must work on daily. Unless you commit yourself to it, you cannot stay motivated. In this section, let's look at simple habits you can follow in your daily life to stay motivated about your goals.

Take a Cold Shower

Whenever you feel demotivated, wash your face with some cold water. If you are at home, take a long, cold shower. A cold shower can quickly jolt you awake and clear your mind. It also helps improve your overall energy levels. As soon as the cold water hits your skin, your body's natural stress response is triggered. During this period, stay calm for 10 to 15 seconds, control your breathing, and try to silence your mind. After these 15 seconds, you will notice that the shower isn't as bad as you thought it initially would be. You will feel awake and energized even if you stay under a cold shower for a minute.

Review Your Goals

Don't forget to review your goals daily. No, it differs from obsessing about them. It merely means you must consciously analyze all the tasks you accomplished on any given day. While doing this, assume a neutral perspective and don't be judgmental. If you notice there is scope for improvement, then you can always work on it.

Start Reading

Reading the stories of successful people can motivate you. Spend some time and read self-development or business books. Learn to feed your mind with positive messages, and you will feel more empowered. You can also stumble upon invaluable lessons from reading such books. By reading, you are consciously shifting your mind to focus on a growth mindset. Reading is also a great way to relax after a stressful day. If you are not keen on reading, then there's no time like the present to develop this habit. Even reading for about 15 minutes in the morning can motivate you. If not, reading, maybe you can watch some inspirational videos.

Your Environment Matters

Regardless of what you want to believe, the environment you spend your time and influences your motivation levels. Your environment influences the way you think, feel, and behave. Your environment consists of the company you keep and the direct environment like your workplace or home. Your environment can either support your goals or prevent you from accomplishing anything in life. For instance, if those around you are distracting you from working, then you cannot get anything done at work. Eventually, you will lose all interest and motivation to keep working.

- Who are the people who support and inspire you?

- Are you around people who hold you back?

- Who are the ones that make me feel better?

- Who are the ones that make you feel worse?

- Do you learn anything from the people you spend time with?

- Does your usual circle drain you out of your energy?

Your answers to these questions will help you understand whether you are spending your time in a good company or not. If you are around toxic people who hold you back, then you cannot become successful. So, pay attention to the company you keep. If your gut tells you something is off, it will do you good to listen to that inner voice!

Conclusion

If you are tired of living your life with no purpose or feel like you're wasting your precious resources, then it is time to set some goals for yourself. You can set professional, personal, health, fitness, lifestyle, or any other goals you want to. The sky is the limit when it comes to setting goals. However, ensure that the goals you set are in sync with your values and vision in life. The different tips and steps you can follow to do this have been discussed in this book in great detail. This book is the ideal guide anyone could use to turn their life around.

In this book, you were given all the information you require to set goals and develop plans and actions to attain those goals. You no longer have to depend on willpower or motivation to attain your goals. Long gone are the days when people believed these two factors were quintessential for attaining goals. By following the simple, actionable tips and steps in this book, you can attain the success you have always desired.

Using the different lazy goal setting hacks in this book and the tips to understand your reasons for setting a specific goal, you can improve your chances of success. Use vision boards and mind mapping for improving your clarity of the goals you have set. Follow the different tips to improve focus, motivation, and self-discipline in this book, and you will see a positive change in your overall life, not just your life but even your attitude toward life. You no longer have to sit by and watch life as it passes you by. Using the actionable tips and steps in this book, you can assume a proactive approach to life instead of a passive one. However, your job doesn't end after you attain your goal. Setting and attaining goals is a lifelong journey. So, keep at it until you have carved out the future you always wished for. Unlock the secrets to setting goals by using the information in this book.

Remember that the key to your successful life lies in your hands. You have the power to turn your life around for the better. You can have the kind of life you want to. The only obstacle you must overcome is your mindset. So, what are you waiting for? All that is left for you to do is to get started *right away.*

Part 2: Procrastination

Discover How to Cure Laziness, Overcome Bad Habits, Develop Motivation, Improve Self-Discipline, Adopt a Success Mindset, and Increase Productivity, Even If You Are a Lazy Person

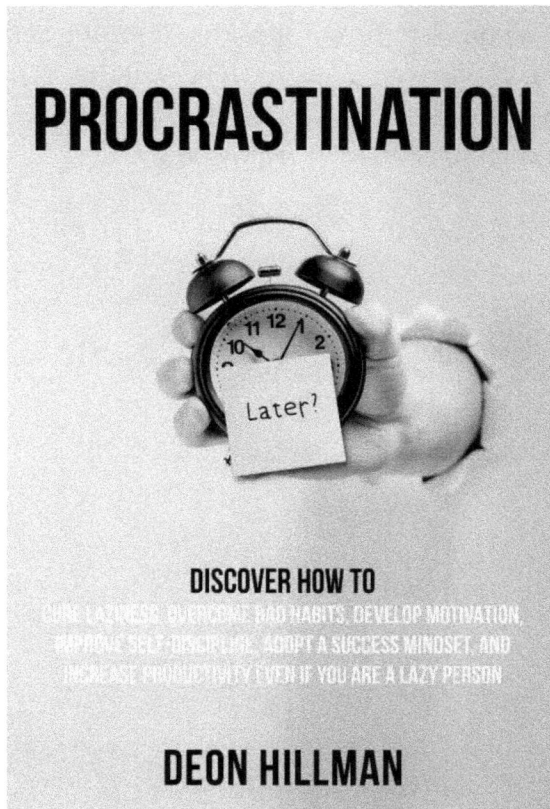

PROCRASTINATION

Later?

DISCOVER HOW TO

CURE LAZINESS, OVERCOME BAD HABITS, DEVELOP MOTIVATION, IMPROVE SELF-DISCIPLINE, ADOPT A SUCCESS MINDSET, AND INCREASE PRODUCTIVITY EVEN IF YOU ARE A LAZY PERSON

DEON HILLMAN

Introduction

Countless books have been written on the subject of procrastination, offering numerous tips and tricks on how to overcome it and create a more successful, productive life. Unfortunately, most of these books fall short of their goal for one reason or another, leaving the reader with little to show for their efforts. Fortunately, this book addresses procrastination in a new and comprehensive way, offering insight into the causes of procrastination in order to provide a deeper understanding of the subject. Furthermore, a clinical evaluation of the psychology behind procrastination will enable you to recognize mindsets and personality traits that impact your productivity from the deepest levels. Subsequently, this book will help you to not just change your habits and behaviors; it will enable you to achieve true personal transformation, the kind that will enable you to pursue and achieve all of your goals, ambitions, and dreams. Finally, the methods and techniques provided will help you to create a clear plan for eliminating procrastination from your life once and for all. By the time you finish reading this book, you will have all the information and tools needed to not only eliminate procrastination, but to live the life you have always desired, one full of purpose, success, and true happiness.

Chapter 1: Why Procrastination Happens

While this book may be the first attempt to solve procrastination for some readers, for many, it will be one of several books they have read on the subject. The question is, why do most books fail to provide significant and effective tools for overcoming procrastination? The most common reason is that they treat procrastination as a singular problem, providing a "one size fits all" perspective that fails to address the numerous causes of procrastination. Since procrastination has many different causes, it stands to reason that it will also have many different cures. Therefore, before you start searching for the methods and tools needed to overcome procrastination once and for all, you must first determine the precise issues that lead to your procrastination in the first place. Believe it or not, there are eight unique behaviors and mindsets that serve to create different forms of procrastination. This chapter will explore each of those mindsets and behaviors, helping you to identify the ones that are keeping you from achieving your goals. As this chapter is focused on the causes of procrastination, it won't discuss the solutions, leaving those for the following chapters where they can be discussed in greater depth.

The Need for Perfection

For many, getting a task or project done simply isn't enough. Instead, they must also achieve perfection. The finished product needs to be the best, or else it's not worth doing. While this perspective may seem to be the stuff of success, the truth of the matter is that the need for perfection is one of the chief causes of procrastination. The more a person requires perfection, the less likely they are to start a project or task for fear that the end result might fall short. Needless to say, this is a significant obstacle to overcome, especially in a world where anything less than perfection is seen as inferior.

The problem with perfection is that it is a virtual impossibility. Almost nothing in life is perfect, which stands to reason. After all, if everything was perfect, then perfection itself would be seen as ordinary, thereby losing its significance. The very fact that perfection is still held as an ideal, underscores its rarity. However, sometimes the problem isn't even with perfection; rather, it is the fear of not being as good as someone else. When you compare your results to the results of others, it can have the effect of making you feel inferior, and that can significantly reduce your desire to start a project seeing as you lack the confidence to achieve a result others will admire.

Perhaps the biggest problem with the need for perfection is the vicious cycle it creates. The fear of falling short will cause you to put off starting a task, which in turn reduces the amount of time you have to complete that task. As the time available shrinks, the chance of achieving success also shrinks, causing you to lose even more confidence, thus procrastinating further still. In the end, the fear of imperfection is often a self-fulfilling prophecy, one that could be largely avoided simply by starting a task or project when you have the most time available to get it done.

Fear of the Unknown

The next cause of procrastination, which affects millions of people, is the fear of the unknown. This fear can present itself in many ways, but more often than not, it takes the form of a fear of disaster. A good example of this is if you ever put off trying a new restaurant because you weren't sure how good their food would be, or whether or not you would have a good time. Although this isn't procrastination as such, it is the same fear of a negative outcome that causes many people to put off actions for as long as possible.

A good example of procrastination due to the fear of the unknown is when a person puts off going to the doctor to get a particular pain or symptom checked out. Many people only go to the doctor when that particular symptom becomes so bad that it impacts their day-to-day lives in a significantly negative way. More often than not, the reason they put off seeing their doctor is the fear of what the doctor might say. Worst case scenarios, including surgery, a terminal diagnosis, or some other extreme result, can flood a person's heart and mind, causing them to put off the appointment until it becomes absolutely necessary.

Needless to say, the results of procrastinating in this way can prove extremely detrimental, especially in the case of a health issue. Modern medicine can cure or at least treat most illnesses when caught in time. Thus, when you procrastinate, you only decrease your chances of getting cured, making this another example of a self-fulfilling prophecy, one that could have been avoided if you had taken prompt action instead of putting things off until the last possible minute.

Delaying for a Better Time

A less sinister cause of procrastination is that of delaying for a better time. How many times have you decided to put off a task or project until later, convincing yourself that you would somehow have more time, energy, or resources at that later moment? Needless to say, there are times when you won't have the right amount of time, energy, or resources to get things done, but this isn't really about that. This is more a matter of waiting for the "right time." And, as most people come to realize at one point or another in their lives, the right time rarely ever comes.

One reason why the right time never comes is that a person's habits rarely change. Thus, if you have low energy on your day off that causes you to put off a task for another day, unless your low energy is the result of a bad night's sleep, sickness, or some other out-of-the-ordinary circumstance, there is no reason to expect your energy levels will be any better the next time around. This leaves you in the very same boat on your next day off, lacking the energy needed to inspire you to address the task or project at hand.

Not having the right amount of money or other resources can also cause a person to put off a project indefinitely, waiting for that golden moment when their life will change, and suddenly they will have more money than usual for no apparent reason. It is one thing if you conscientiously choose to put a project off in order to build up the cash or resources needed to accomplish it. That is simply good planning. What makes it procrastination is when you just expect circumstances to improve without any effort on your part. The simple truth is that the time and resources at your disposal now are probably the same as they will be at any other time, so this is as good a moment to start the task as any.

Choosing Easier Tasks First

Sometimes procrastination can show up in more subtle ways. This is especially true when you have numerous tasks to complete within a given time frame. Ordinarily, procrastination is easy to spot, as it is when you put off the single task or project on your plate for another time. However, in the event that you have more than one project, you can actually procrastinate while still appearing to be productive. This is when you put off the bigger or more daunting project until later, choosing to accomplish the easier, more enjoyable tasks first. Again, even though you are still productive, the act of putting off that larger task is, in fact, a significant form of procrastination.

The problem with this type of procrastination is that it can prove to get worse as time progresses, becoming the proverbial snowball gaining mass as it rolls downhill. More often than not, a person chooses the easier tasks first because they are more fun. Choosing to put off boring or tedious tasks until later won't make them any better. Instead, because you've spent your day doing the fun things first, the task you put off will only seem even more tedious or undesirable later on. This is especially true if the task requires a great deal of energy, since your energy levels will be even more depleted by the time you address the task at the last possible moment.

Another reason why this form of procrastination is perhaps the most dangerous is that you can convince yourself that you aren't actually procrastinating at all. Because you are doing other activities, you feel productive, and therefore you lack the guilt that sheer laziness can create. Unfortunately, more often than not, this "productivity" is merely an illusion. Although the smaller, more enjoyable tasks need to be done, they don't provide the same amount of results as the larger, more tedious projects. Therefore, despite appearing to be productive, the fact is that you are actually wasting as much time as if you weren't doing anything at all.

Low Energy Levels

Any task or project, regardless of how large or small, will require a certain amount of energy to get done. Whether that energy is physical or mental, it can often be tempting to put off a task if you don't feel as though your current energy levels are high enough for what needs to be accomplished.

The bottom line is that your energy levels usually start high and diminish as the day progresses, not the other way around. Therefore, if you feel as though you don't have the energy for something first thing in the morning, you definitely won't have it later in the afternoon. Instead, the longer you put off a task or project for, the lower your energy levels will be by the time you get around to working on that project. This means that you will feel even worse about accomplishing your task, when you are left with no other choice, and you can't put it off any longer.

Stress can play a significant role in this scenario, as well. If you are unmotivated due to the stress of the project or task at hand, putting it off until later will only make matters worse. Now, in addition to being a stressful task, you have the added anxiety of having far less time in which to complete it. Although it can seem like you are doing yourself a favor by putting off the big, unpleasant tasks until later, the longer you delay, the worse things get.

Lack of Direction

So far, the reasons for procrastination have focused on poor decision making, a lack of discipline, and other behaviors that are largely associated with laziness or a lack of motivation. There are, however, some causes that affect even those with rock-solid willpower and unshakable resolve. One such cause is a lack of direction, which is when you don't know exactly where to start on a project, or what direction to take with a specific task. Even when you have all the energy and discipline in the world, if you don't know how to tackle the task at hand, it can make it seem like getting started is all but impossible.

A good way to imagine this is if you are sitting in your car with nowhere to go. You can have all the time in the world and a full tank of gas, but if you don't know where you are supposed to drive next, then there is no reason for you to leave where you are. This is what happens when people don't get thorough, precise directions on how to perform a task or project. Without proper direction, any effort could be wasted, or even worse, prove counterproductive in the long run. Therefore, procrastinating is seen as a safe bet, ensuring no mistakes are made and no effort wasted.

The problem here is that "kicking the can down the road," so to speak, doesn't solve the problem. Sure, taking uncertain action isn't the best plan either, but doing nothing will only ensure that the situation fails to improve. Putting off action while trying to find direction is one thing, but simply putting off action isn't going to get the job done. Therefore, this is one of those areas where recognizing the cause of procrastination can make all the difference. Once you get the direction you need, the procrastination will be instantly solved, allowing you to accomplish the task at hand without further delay.

Constant Distractions

Perhaps the most common cause of procrastination is the constant barrage of distractions that affect everyone at all times. Everything from cell phones to radios, TVs, and other sources of noise and entertainment can tempt even the strongest willed person away from the task they are performing, causing them to delay their efforts "just for a little while." Unfortunately, the sheer number of distractions available can make "just a little while" turn into hours or even days in extreme cases. The bottom line is that everyone's mind wants to have fun and is therefore easily tempted away from any work when a more enjoyable alternative presents itself.

However, not all distractions have to be pleasant in nature. The truth of the matter is that there are just as many work-related distractions as there are distractions of any other kind. Constant phone calls, people interrupting to ask questions, and even more work being added to your inbox, can distract your attention and effort more than your cell phone ever could. The problem in these cases is that since they are work-related, such distractions are seen as acceptable, making procrastination almost justified. Needless to say, no matter what form procrastination takes, the end result is always the same—putting off accomplishing the task at hand, thereby reducing efficiency, overall productivity, and the quality of the results.

Fear of Commitment

The eighth and final cause of procrastination to consider is the fear of commitment. This is when you know how much time and energy a particular project will take, making it overwhelming in scope. Fear of commitment is probably the main reason why just about everyone has that big project that they just never get around to. Whether it's painting your house, cleaning out your basement, or replacing your old, worn-out deck, any project that will require large amounts of cash, time, and effort, is one that can easily be pushed back to another time.

This is another case where procrastination isn't necessarily the result of bad habits or a negative mindset. Instead, the sheer scope of some projects can make them overwhelming for anyone, even the most inspired and energetic of people. The real problem here is that when such a large project is treated as a single entity, it can seem insurmountable. As a result, such projects get put off for one reason or another, until they either become an absolute necessity or they just get canceled altogether.

Chapter 2: The Psychology of Procrastination

Most books and videos that try to address the root causes of procrastination tend to approach things in terms of behavior and habits. Poor time management, a lack of discipline, an inability to avoid distractions and the like, are usually cited as the critical issues when it comes to the causes of procrastination in its various forms. However, recent studies have shown that there is another dimension to procrastination, one that affects people on a deeper level. That dimension is the psychology of procrastination. This approach argues that elements such as self-esteem, guilt, thrill-seeking behavior, and fear of failure contribute not only to procrastination but also to the other behaviors and habits that are usually seen as the cause. This chapter will explore the psychology of procrastination, showing how many of the behaviors that are commonly seen as causes are, in fact, the symptoms of a greater issue.

Situational vs. Chronic

In order to effectively address the issue of procrastination, the first thing you need to ask yourself is what kind of procrastinator you are. The simple truth of the matter is that just about everyone procrastinates at one time or another, meaning that procrastination itself isn't a rare or dangerous behavior as such. However, studies done by psychology professor Joseph Ferrari at DePaul University, have determined that as many as twenty percent of people are what can be considered "chronic procrastinators." These are the people who procrastinate on a regular basis, regardless of the task or project at hand. In contrast, the remaining eighty percent of people simply put things off from time to time, usually for reasons that are easy to understand, such as low motivation, feeling overwhelmed, or a lack of time and resources. Therefore, before you start trying to change your behaviors, the first thing you need to do is determine how serious your procrastination really is.

If you are a situational procrastinator, then you will feel pretty confident when it comes to getting things done on time on a regular basis. Furthermore, you probably won't have any issues with getting started on a project or task, as you will have the confidence and motivation needed to get things rolling without delay. When it comes to the large, undesirable projects such as painting your house or going to the doctor, you might struggle with maintaining your usual discipline and starting in a responsible and timely manner. In this case, the basic methods for overcoming procrastination will be enough to change your behavior on those rare occasions, helping you to raise your game and be more consistent in your ability to tackle any task or project with confidence and determination.

Alternatively, if you are a chronic procrastinator, then you know that the rare occurrence is when you address a task or project in a timely and responsible manner, not when you put it off for another time. For one reason or another, you struggle to find the motivation to start things off on the right foot. Day after day sees you put things off to the last minute, thereby increasing your stress, decreasing your performance, and even undermining your chances of success. Eventually, your reputation suffers, and you are left living a life far beneath your true potential. If this describes the situation you find yourself in, then you are a chronic procrastinator. Numerous studies around the world have concluded that this chronic condition is the result of psychological issues that need to be addressed at the root. Fortunately, these studies have also broken down the various psychological explanations into a few groups that are easy to recognize, and thus easy to manage and even overcome.

Arousal Procrastination

The first type of procrastination to consider is that of arousal procrastination. This is the form of procrastination most commonly associated with extreme thrill-seekers. Ordinary thrill-seekers might choose to go skydiving for fun, enjoying the rush as they freefall from a plane before deploying their parachute and safely returning to the ground. In contrast, extreme thrill seekers will not only go skydiving; they will wait until the very last second before deploying their parachute, putting their lives at even greater risk in the process. The need for that extra adrenaline rush makes them take already considerable challenges and add another layer of danger to them. Such people may not even be aware of their need for this adrenaline rush, resulting in them being a victim to their addiction and the behaviors associated with it.

In terms of procrastination, arousal procrastinators will put off big, important tasks or projects until the last minute in order to feel that exhilaration of staring disaster in the face. Ordinary people would get started on such projects as early as possible, thus ensuring a safe timeframe within which to get the project done. This is like the ordinary person deploying their parachute as soon as possible in order to ensure their safety while skydiving. However, the same rush that comes from deploying the parachute at the last minute is the rush that comes from delivering a mere project seconds before the deadline expires. This gives them the experience of escaping destruction each and every day without having to go to the lengths of going skydiving or performing some other death-defying activity.

What makes this form of procrastination unique is that it isn't the result of self-destructive behavior or low self-esteem. Nor is it the byproduct of laziness or a poor work ethic. Instead, it is the result of an addiction to the adrenaline that accompanies high levels of anxiety, usually associated with life and death scenarios. This is why many methods of overcoming procrastination fall short of producing results for arousal procrastinators, as they don't address the true cause of their behavior.

Avoider Procrastination

The second form of procrastination to consider is that of avoider procrastination. This is perhaps the most common of all forms, and it is what keeps most people from achieving their full potential. Simply put, someone in this category will avoid performing a task or project for as long as possible because they are afraid of the outcome. More often than not, this is reduced to a basic fear of failure. While the fear of failure does play a large role in avoider procrastination, it is not the only form of fear that is present. In fact, many studies have shown that the fear of success also contributes to avoider procrastination. Therefore, if you find that you avoid doing things until the last minute for fear of one type or another, then this is the form of procrastination that impacts you.

Needless to say, failure is something that most people want to avoid at all costs. As a result, if you feel as though you aren't up to the task at hand, a fear of failure will cause you to put off that task for as long as possible, thereby avoiding the issue and the failure it threatens to bring. This usually stems from low self-esteem, meaning that you feel inadequate for the task you have been given.

The stronger your fear of failure, the longer you will avoid performing the task at hand. In this case, however, most people do bring themselves to tackle the project, usually successfully, just in the nick of time.

Another form of avoider procrastination addresses the fear of failure in a more self-destructive way. This is when instead of overcoming the fear of failure and accomplishing the task, you actually sabotage your efforts, failing to complete the task or project in the time given. More often than not, this is an attempt to shift the blame from your perceived inadequacies to the lack of time available as a result of your procrastination. What makes this form worse is that the fear of failure is so absolute that the individual simply refuses to take any chance at all. Rather than trying to accomplish the task or project, they actually create a situation where failure is guaranteed. Known as "self-handicapping," this is a behavior that results from the lowest levels of self-esteem and self-confidence.

Finally, there is the fear of success, something that most people don't even realize exists. There are two main reasons for fearing success. First, there is the fear that by succeeding, you will invite greater expectations on your performance. In other words, when you go above and beyond, delivering results against all the odds, you will be expected to maintain that level of effort on a regular basis. This stands to reason as most companies come to expect the best from their employees. Therefore, once you demonstrate your best, you open the flood gates for your boss to expect that level of performance each and every time. This will only increase your workload, and thus your day-to-day stress. Subsequently, you avoid putting your best foot forward since the consequences of success are seemingly negative in nature.

The second reason why a person fears success is that they don't want to make others look bad. This usually takes place in competitive environments where kind-hearted people can't stand the thought of being the reason others lose out. Rather than achieving success at the expense of others, such a person will avoid a task or project, reducing their chances of success as a result. It's a bit like faking an injury to allow someone else to win the race. This type of procrastination is pretty rare, but it is no less detrimental than any of the other forms. The overall result is a reduction of effort, thereby keeping you from achieving the success you are actually capable of.

Decisional Procrastination

Decisional procrastination affects both situational and chronic procrastinators alike. In short, it is when you avoid a task or project because you either don't know enough to make the right decision to get started, or you simply can't handle the responsibility of making decisions because you are afraid of making a mistake. In the end, the fear of making bad decisions that lead to failure will cause a person to commit decisional procrastination for as long as possible.

In the situational case, this is usually the result of being unclear about the task at hand. A lack of instruction, training, or general direction can undermine a person's confidence when it comes to knowing where to start. This doesn't necessarily mean that the individual is suffering from low self-esteem; rather, it means that they find themselves in a situation where uncertainty creates the fear of getting things wrong. By procrastinating, they can avoid making those decisions, thereby burying their head in the sand for a while, hoping the situation will resolve itself by some magic or miracle. Unfortunately, such magic and miracles are usually not forthcoming, meaning that the individual is left to face their demons later on, whether they like it or not.

In the case of a chronic procrastinator, decisional procrastination comes from a lack of confidence when making decisions. Thus, instead of this being a one-off situation, it is one that occurs on a regular basis. Most people in this category simply can't handle the stress of being responsible for the outcome of any decision they have to make. Therefore, they avoid making decisions as often and for as long as possible. Although many bring themselves to make those painful decisions at the last moment, some will procrastinate long enough to ensure failure rather than take the chance of causing the failure with the decisions they would have had to make. This allows them to blame their failure on a lack of time, thereby absolving them of any personal blame.

The Role of Guilt in Procrastinating

The final thing to consider is the role that guilt plays when it comes to procrastination. Regardless of the type of procrastination a person practices, one thing that just about all procrastinators share is the feeling of guilt. More often than not, this guilt is seen as a consequence of procrastination. However, recent studies have discovered a startling new angle, one that suggests that rather than being the consequence of procrastination, guilt can actually be the cause. This means that it's the guilt that leads to self-destructive behavior, not the other way around.

Doctor David Maloney is a psychotherapist who has explored the many causes of procrastination. In addition to the common psychological causes, namely low self-esteem or the fear of failure, he has discovered that guilt can cause a person to procrastinate, even to the point of failing to finish a task or project altogether. His conclusion is that this behavior is a form of self-punishment, the sabotaging of success due to guilt or some other emotional trauma that can be traced to the individual's past. Only by recognizing the source of that guilt or trauma can a person effectively end the self-destructive behavior and begin to achieve the success they both desire and deserve.

In order to identify most causes of procrastination, you need to ask yourself why you are avoiding the task at hand. However, in this case, the question you would ask is why you feel undeserving of the success within your reach. After all, that is the overall reason for this type of procrastination—the deliberate self-sabotaging in order to prevent yourself from achieving success. Only by searching your history, including all emotional traumas and other events that could explain your feeling of guilt, can you find the reason you feel unworthy of living a life of success and happiness. Once you have that piece of the puzzle, all procrastination habits and behaviors will disappear as your subconscious mind won't need them any longer. After all, once the guilt has resolved, the need for punishment will no longer exist.

Reasons for this type of self-sabotage can come in all different forms. For example, if you cheated in order to win in the past, you might feel guilty of the success you achieved, thereby causing you to surrender current and future successes in order to atone for your wrongdoing. This sense of atonement can also be the result of hurting others in the past due to being overly competitive, or the guilt of seeing someone suffer as the result of your success, even if you didn't do anything wrong. All in all, this type of guilt usually has the effect of taking the joy out of success, thereby causing a person to avoid success at all costs.

Another reason behind guilt-driven procrastination is the need to make things harder on yourself, which can stem from a feeling of always having an advantage over others, such as being favored or having more resources at your disposal. In order to assuage your guilt for having such an advantage, you procrastinate, thereby undermining your chances of success. This creates a more level playing field in your mind, thus making the game fairer. In the end, the sense of guilt can always be traced to an issue of self-esteem, one that you feel can only be corrected by punishment. Subsequently, the only cure for guilt-driven procrastination is to forgive yourself for any past mistakes or any sense of entitlement, so that you can get on with achieving the success you are capable of.

Chapter 3: Procrastination vs. Laziness

One of the biggest problems when it comes to overcoming procrastination is that most books address procrastination as a symptom of laziness. The common belief is that anyone who is properly motivated will naturally tackle any task or project without delay, thereby avoiding any type of procrastination. Alternatively, when someone puts off tasks or projects, it suggests that they lack initiative, energy, or ambition. At best, they lack the desire to grow and succeed; at worst, they are downright lazy. Surprisingly enough, the link between laziness and procrastination is often unwarranted. In fact, one is a matter of personality, whereas the other is a matter of behavior. Ignoring this fundamental truth can result in misdiagnosing an individual as being lazy simply for putting off the task or project at hand. Therefore, in order to properly recognize the root cause of procrastination, it is vital to first understand the difference between laziness and procrastination. Only then can you begin to take the proper steps to overcome procrastination within your life once and for all.

Personality vs. Behavior

As already mentioned, the biggest difference between procrastination and laziness is that one is a matter of personality, whereas the other is a matter of behavior. This is a distinction that most people fail to understand, causing them to assume the two conditions are one and the same, when, in fact, nothing could be further from the truth. The best way to understand the difference between personality and behavior is to see personality as who a person is and behavior as what a person does. Although at first glance, these concepts might appear to be virtually identical, upon closer inspection, their differences become abundantly clear.

Who you are as a person can have a number of influences. First and foremost are your genetics. Long-term studies—like the Minnesota Twin Family Study undertaken by the University of Minnesota—have revealed that personality traits can be passed from generation to generation, even becoming stronger with each generation. A good way to portray this would be in terms of physical strength. Although a person can develop physical strength by going to the gym and working out, they can also inherit a certain "natural strength," one that is the consequence of having a family history of strong men and women in their family tree. Thus, a person may grow up to have a certain level of strength simply because of the nature of their genetic makeup.

Additionally, strength can be the result of environmental conditions such as upbringing. Children who have to perform physical labor from an early age will grow up to be physically stronger than those who grow up in less physically demanding circumstances. The strength such a child possesses later in life will be of a more natural sort, one that they don't have to maintain through exercise as such. This makes their strength a part of who they are, rather than the consequence of what they do.

In contrast, a behavior is when a person chooses to perform an action in order to achieve a particular result. When a person chooses to go to the gym and work out, they are performing the behavior that will make them strong. In time they may be as strong if not stronger than the person who is strong due to genetics or upbringing. However, they will have to work at developing and maintaining that strength. Once they stop exercising and working out, their body will return to its natural state, thereby losing the strength they have developed by going to the gym.

This is how personality and behavior works. Personality is who a person is inherent. Since procrastination is behavior by definition, no one is a natural procrastinator. They might be a poor decision-maker or have low self-esteem, but the procrastination itself will be a symptom of those traits, not the trait itself. Laziness, in contrast, is a personality trait, one that can be passed down through genetics, or developed by environmental factors such as upbringing. As such, laziness isn't the action itself; rather, it is the personality trait behind the action. This is why highly motivated people can procrastinate, and why a typically lazy person may jump in and work on a task without delay. Fortunately, once you determine whether you suffer from a matter of personality or behavior, laziness or procrastination, you can take the necessary steps to change your direction and begin achieving the success you both desire and deserve.

The True Nature of Laziness

If you look up the word "laziness" in the dictionary, you will find that it refers to a general disinclination to perform any kind of work or chore that would require significant effort. The Latin root for laziness is "indolentia," which describes a mindset that lacks trouble or pain. This underscores the previous point that laziness is a personality trait as opposed to behavior. Putting off work or avoiding work is the behavior, but the desire to do so is the mindset, and that is what makes all the difference.

A 2012 study by researchers at Vanderbilt University, which was published in the *Journal of Neuroscience*, showed that lazy people actually have a different neurological makeup to the average person. Everyone is driven by a chemical reaction to stimuli, resulting in making something desirable or undesirable. Exercise is a good example of this phenomenon. Almost everyone experiences a release of dopamine when eating certain foods or participating in sexual activity. Dopamine is a chemical produced in the body that causes a feeling of pleasure. However, while most people also get that release of dopamine during and after exercising, "lazy" people do not. This means that rather than having a positive mental and emotional impact, exercise takes on an undesirable nature. The result is that people who are lazy simply avoid exercise as it fails to provide any pleasurable incentive.

Although this may seem strange, it isn't very hard to understand when you consider just how pleasure-driven the average person really is. You can see this in the foods that people eat. The main reason why so many people are overweight is that they eat foods heavy in fat, sugar, or salt. This is because those foods taste good, meaning they get pleasure from eating them. Just as eating raw broccoli doesn't provide that same feeling of pleasure and bliss to the average eater, so too, does work and exercise fail to provide a sense of contentment or pleasure for a lazy person. As a result, people who are lazy avoid work the same way as the average person avoids eating a salad for lunch.

This is where the main difference between procrastination and laziness comes into play. Whereas a procrastinator has good intentions at first, a lazy person lacks any intention of getting things done. Thus, rather than putting something off for another time, or avoiding a task until the last possible minute, a lazy person won't sign on for that task in the first place. Instead, they will avoid any work altogether, always finding shortcuts and loopholes that allow them to put in the least amount of effort necessary. In fact, lazy people often spend more effort trying to avoid a task than the task would have actually required in the first place. However, since the task promises pain and unhappiness, any amount of effort is worthwhile if it helps them to avoid having to do the task.

Another way to imagine this is to give yourself the choice of going to the beach or going to the dentist. No one in their right mind would ever choose to go to the dentist over the beach. Going to the beach is a win for anyone. This is exactly how a lazy person's mindset works. Anything and everything that resembles work is a trip to the dentist for them. No good ever comes of it, only pain and misery. Therefore, they conscientiously choose to do no work since that way they can avoid the pain and misery. No effort is too great if it spares them a trip to the proverbial dentist. Thus, they will put themselves in a position where they can consistently avoid work, putting in as little effort as possible just to get by.

Fortunately, even though laziness is a personality trait, one that has been shown to be genetic, as well as the result of environmental conditions, it is something that can be overcome. Just as the risk for any hereditary physical illness that runs in the family can be reduced by taking appropriate action, so too, can appropriate actions be taken to develop better habits that overcome the tendency of laziness. The key is to recognize the fact that your behavior is the result of laziness so that you can be sure the actions you take are effective. The best way to be sure is to ask yourself the following questions:

- Do you avoid any and all kinds of work?
- Does work make you feel exhausted?
- Do you lack a sense of satisfaction when you finish a task or project?
- Do you feel less energized after exercising?
- Are you likely to avoid even the simplest of tasks for no reason?

If you answered "yes" to most or all of these questions, then you aren't struggling with procrastination, rather you are struggling with laziness. Fortunately, this book will provide proven methods for overcoming laziness and creating habits that will enable you to live a more productive, successful life, one that brings you the happiness you deserve.

The True Nature of Procrastination

Unlike laziness, procrastination is not the act of avoiding any type of work or labor altogether. Instead, procrastination has a very different meaning, one that involves time as opposed to effort. The Latin root of the word literally means to put off until tomorrow. This fits the general understanding of the term, namely the act of pushing a task or project as far back as possible. Although some forms of procrastination can result in failing to complete a task or project, most simply result in the task or project not being completed until the last possible minute. This makes a huge difference in terms of the mindset and personality of someone who procrastinates compared to someone who is inherently lazy. And this is why procrastination and laziness need to be treated as very different conditions.

One of the first things to note is that procrastination is a behavior, not a personality trait or a mindset. It is an action, not a state of being. As such, it can be caused by such things as poor habits, a lack of direction, or any number of issues that can easily be resolved. Someone who procrastinates, therefore, isn't necessarily "broken" or in need of a major overhaul. Instead, they just need to break some bad habits and replace them with better, more productive habits. This makes the process a lot easier, as the mindset of a procrastinator is usually positive in nature, meaning that better habits will take hold quickly and start producing results right away.

However, the first step is to determine whether or not you are a procrastinator, as opposed to being lazy. As mentioned before, people who are lazy lack the intention of doing any work at all. In contrast, a procrastinator tends to have the best intentions. They take on a list of projects or tasks with the expectation of completing them, thereby achieving success and satisfaction as a result. This goes back to the studies conducted that determined the role dopamine plays in a person's work ethic. Usually people tend to feel satisfaction and pleasure from accomplishing goals. Even if they have to put in vast amounts of effort and time to accomplish a task, they will feel as though it was worth it in the end. In fact, the harder the task, the greater the sense of accomplishment the individual experiences when it is finally completed. Therefore, rather than avoiding work completely, a procrastinator will eagerly accept a task at first, only to put off working on it later on.

When a procrastinator puts off a task or project, they usually fill their time with less important tasks and projects, thereby still maintaining some level of productivity. Alternatively, laziness leads people to avoid a task or project and spend their time being idle and unproductive, thereby producing no results at all. This is perhaps the best proof that a person who procrastinates isn't actually lazy, rather they are uninspired or overwhelmed, resulting in them losing confidence in a task rather than lacking the desire to see it completed.

A good way to see this difference is to revisit the example of going to the dentist or going to the beach. The lazy person will choose to go to the beach every single time, without ever giving the dentist a second thought. Alternatively, the procrastinator might actually choose the dentist on occasion, even if they put it off for as long as possible due to their fear of the experience. Or, they might experience a feeling of guilt each time they choose the beach, eventually causing them to choose the dentist as they know that is the right choice to make. This is how they view work. Although part of them is drawn to the easier path, they have a sense of responsibility that prevents them from shirking work altogether. No matter how undesirable the task or project proves to be, a procrastinator will almost always get to it in the end, as they know it is the right thing to do. Fortunately, this inherent sense of value means that procrastinators aren't afraid of work or effort; they are simply afraid of getting started on a particular task or project in a timely way. Thus, a simple tweaking of habits and perspectives is all it takes to overcome procrastination.

In order to determine whether or not you struggle with procrastination, as opposed to laziness, simply ask yourself the following questions:

- Do you generally enjoy being productive?

- Does work give you a sense of purpose?

- Do you feel a sense of satisfaction when you finish a project?

- Do you usually feel energized and refreshed after exercising?

- Do you usually accomplish all your tasks on a regular basis?

If you answered "yes" to most or all of these questions, then you are not lazy. Instead, you are a regular individual who struggles to face those large and unpleasant projects in a timely manner. Fortunately, the solution to this situation is fairly easy and straightforward, meaning that you can fix your behaviors and begin enjoying a more productive and satisfying life as a result.

Chapter 4: Steps to Curing Procrastination

The process of curing procrastination is a relatively straightforward one. However, it is comprised of numerous steps that must be followed in a particular order and to their fullest. What causes most people to fall short when it comes to overcoming procrastination is that they simply jump in and perform a few steps at random without any rhyme or reason. In a way, this would be like trying to bake a cake without following the recipe. Even if you use the right ingredients, unless you perform the steps in their proper order, you will fail to create anything worthwhile. However, when you use the right ingredients and follow each and every step carefully, you will create a perfect, delicious cake. Likewise, when you follow the steps for overcoming procrastination in their precise order, you will give yourself the best possible chance for success, enabling you to overcome procrastination once and for all. This chapter will address the various steps, providing a brief overview that will be elaborated upon in further chapters. By understanding the nature and order of these steps, you will be able to take control of your life and start achieving the success you so desperately desire.

Understand Your Reasons for Procrastinating

The first step to overcoming procrastination is to understand the reasons for your procrastination in the first place. This can be likened to you trying to find a cure for insomnia. Simply knowing that you are sleep deprived isn't enough when it comes to solving the problem. After all, there are numerous reasons for sleep deprivation, including not setting aside enough time for sleep, sleeping in a bright room, too much noise, a bad mattress, or high levels of stress and anxiety. Changing your mattress won't cure your lack of sleep if you aren't setting aside enough time to sleep each and every night. Nor would taking supplements help if you slept in a loud and bright room. Only when you identify the cause of your sleep deprivation can you take the proper steps to overcome it. Thus, if you knew you had a bad mattress, then replacing it would ensure you got better sleep, as would adding more time each night if that were needed.

This is how overcoming procrastination needs to be addressed. While you might get lucky if you simply jump in and start trying all of the methods randomly, the chances are you will only experience nominal results. This will probably cause you to fall short of creating any lasting and effective habits, as you won't get the results you need. However, when you take the time to carefully examine the true nature of your procrastination, you will be able to identify specific causes, each of which has a unique cure. By applying the cures that address your specific issues, you can ensure success in overcoming procrastination once and for all.

The first few chapters of this book cover the process of discovering the true nature of your procrastination, including whether it is behavioral or the result of your personality. No matter the cause, there is a guaranteed method or approach that will help you to change your behavior, and thus create a more productive life, one that allows you to achieve success on a regular basis. It is vital, however, that you take the time to carefully examine your situation. This is also true in the event that you try a particular method that proves less effective than you expect. Sometimes procrastination can have more than one cause, so if one cure only provides slight relief, the trick is to reevaluate your situation and look for other potential causes. Writing down your thoughts, efforts, and results in a journal, is a sure way to increase your chances of success. This will allow you to track your progress, noting which methods worked better and which ones failed to achieve the results you hoped for.

Identify Any Negative Thoughts and Change Them

One of the most common causes of procrastination is a negative mindset. This stands to reason, as the expectation of pain or pleasure can influence a person's behavior. If you tell a child that if they get their homework done, you will take them to get some ice cream, they will work like a maniac in order to get their reward. However, if you tell the same child that when they finish their homework, you will let them mow the lawn, suddenly the incentive to get their work done disappears. This isn't laziness, nor is it some self-destructive mindset that keeps the child from achieving success. Instead, it is a matter of stimulus. Positive rewards will encourage a person to pursue the goal that provides those rewards, whereas a lack of reward, or even worse, a painful outcome will cause a person to delay or even avoid the goals that lead to those less desirable outcomes.

Unfortunately, many of the undesirable outcomes that people predict are self-created. Failure, for example, is never guaranteed. Yet, most procrastinators have it in their mind that the task or project at hand will somehow lead to failure, thereby causing them negative results. This causes them to delay or avoid those tasks and projects, which ultimately leads to the failure they were afraid of in the first place. The trick is to identify any negative thoughts and to change them, thereby creating a more positive mindset in the process. In the case of the fear of failure, you would take the vision of failing and replace it with one of actually achieving the goal at hand. Thus, rather than having your mind filled with images of ridicule and embarrassment, you would fill your mind with images of happiness, validation, and even praise from your peers. This is how you remove the negative expectation that causes procrastination, and replace it with a positive expectation, one that encourages action and gives you all the inspiration you need to accomplish any task or project.

Confront Laziness

Another significant cause of procrastination is laziness. What sets this cause apart from all others is that laziness is a personality trait, not a behavior. Therefore, procrastination caused by laziness isn't as simple to fix as procrastination caused by disorganization. Instead, it will take a great deal more time and effort to get a handle on, to begin to change in a real and meaningful way. Fortunately, the steps for achieving this goal are proven and relatively straightforward. The key is to follow them precisely and to commit to them for as long as it takes.

In order to understand laziness and how it can be cured, it is necessary to understand the relationship between personality and behavior. Any behavior can be learned, which means that any bad behavior can be unlearned and replaced with a better one. However, this is only true in the case of behaviors not associated with personality. In the case of those directly influenced by personality, it isn't enough to simply change the behavior. Instead, you need to take the necessary steps to change your personality at its core, thereby changing all of your behaviors in the process because personality directly influences behavior.

Fortunately, although the process of changing your personality will require time and effort, it is fairly straight forward in nature. Simply put, the trick is to turn the equation around. Thus, instead of letting your personality affect your behavior, you start letting your behavior influence your personality. By engaging in more positive behavior on a grand scale, you can virtually rewrite how your mind works, changing everything from how you perceive work to how you perceive life itself. Therefore, once you start to exchange bad behaviors for good ones, you will start to notice a shift in how you think and feel overall. This shift will continue as you practice better behaviors and habits until, eventually, your personality will have evolved. Eventually, you will replace laziness with a sense of purpose, and this new personality will influence all of your choices and behaviors, helping you to live a better life in every possible way.

Organize Your Life

Chaos is another element that keeps countless people from fulfilling their full potential and thus achieving the success they deserve. This can come in several different ways, including a chaotic schedule, a chaotic work environment, and even a chaotic state of mind. More often than not, one manifestation of chaos will lead to the others, meaning that a chaotic schedule can spill over into a chaotic work environment and mindset. Fortunately, the reverse is also true, meaning that when you start to eliminate chaos in one area, you find that the other areas follow suit.

The simplest way to overcome chaos is to organize your life. Whether you choose to do this from the outside in, or the inside out, doesn't matter as such. What matters the most is that you approach this in the way that works best for you. Thus, you might choose to address your workspace, clearing the clutter, and organizing the things that need to remain. As you master the art of organizing your physical space, you will begin to notice that your thoughts, emotions, and other non-physical elements also become better organized. Eventually, you will regain control over your life, eliminating chaos and all the negative consequences it brings.

One such consequence is procrastination. The fact is that a lack of organization can cause even the most dedicated and hard-working person to put off tasks and projects until a better time. Unfortunately, that better time rarely comes. However, once the individual restores order to their life, both in physical and non-physical terms, then their tendency to procrastinate will virtually disappear, along with the chaos and confusion that plagued them. The dynamic for organizing your life is very similar to that of overcoming laziness, in that bringing organization to your behaviors and actions will, in turn, bring organization to your personality. This will begin to influence all of your behaviors in a positive way, removing the blocks that keep you from achieving your full potential.

Break Down Large Projects into Smaller Tasks

Most causes of procrastination stem from the individual in question. This is true when the cause is due to behavior or personality. Laziness, a disorganized lifestyle, and even the fear of failure, are all part of the individual rather than the circumstances they face. However, there are times when procrastination is the result of the task or project at hand, rather than anything to do with the person facing that task or project. In such a case, the way to overcome procrastination is to change the nature of the task or project, not to change the individual. Fortunately, this process is one of the easiest to perform, and it usually requires little more than a fresh approach, which turns even the most daunting project into something desirable and easy to achieve.

One of the best examples of this is to break down large projects into smaller tasks. Sometimes what causes a person to put off a project is the sheer size of the undertaking. Such things as painting a house or building a deck can seem far too complex, making even the most honest and hardworking person put off the project for as long as possible. Most of the time, a person will put off a large project because they lack the time or energy to complete the entire job. The idea is that they might have more time or energy later on down the road. Unfortunately, this is rarely the case. More often than not, the amount of time and energy you have available now is the same amount that you will have in the future. Therefore, the trick is not to make your resources grow, but to make your project shrink. When you break down a large project into smaller, more manageable tasks, you make it possible to accomplish each smaller task with the time and energy you have at your disposal. Eventually, as you knock out one task after another, you begin to accomplish the big project as a whole. Additionally, you will be less likely to avoid the smaller tasks, thereby eliminating procrastination once and for all.

Create Good Habits

The final step to overcoming procrastination is to create good habits. This makes a whole lot of sense when you consider that most forms of procrastination are the result of bad habits and behaviors in the first place. Whether those bad habits are the consequence of laziness, poor time management, low self-esteem, or any similar condition, the bottom line is that once they are replaced with better habits, the negative consequences will be replaced with positive results. In the end, a person's actions are what defines them, not their thoughts, or even their personality. Subsequently, by creating good habits, you achieve greater success and begin to live the life of your dreams.

One of the most critical elements in the creation of good habits is to keep a journal. This will enable you to do three things. First, it will enable you to write down the challenges you face. Once you have your "demons" down on paper, you will begin to feel more in control of your life right away. This will give you the courage needed to face those demons and to begin improving your habits, and thus your life. The second thing is that it enables you to write down the changes you want to make. Thus, if your bad habit is to oversleep, your desired change might be to go to bed earlier, or to simply get up the first time your alarm goes off. Writing this down will help you to commit to the solution, thereby increasing your chances of success. The third thing a journal enables you to do is to track your progress. If your initial efforts fall short, you can see why, and this will help you to make changes that will improve your results. Therefore, if you are serious about overcoming procrastination once and for all, it is essential that you keep a journal in which you record every aspect of your journey.

The best thing about creating good habits is that those habits will begin to improve who you are as a person. As mentioned earlier, personality directly influences behavior. That said, behavior can also directly affect personality. Therefore, each and every good habit you form will improve your personality in some unique way. The more good habits you create, the greater that improvement will become. Eventually, not only will you have achieved your goal of overcoming procrastination, you will also have achieved an element of personal development that will affect every area of your life. This will lead not just to greater productivity but also to higher self-esteem, a more positive mindset, and a general sense of self-confidence, which will enable you to chase after those goals that help you turn your life into the life of your dreams.

Chapter 5: Tweaking Your Thoughts to Avoid Procrastination

The human mind is nothing short of a miracle. Capable of conceiving everything from art to technology, the power of the mind is quite literally beyond measure. Interestingly enough, in addition to creating art and technology, the human mind also creates the way a person sees the world around them. In a way, it could be said that the mind creates reality itself. Thus, if a person's mind is positive in nature, then the result will be that their reality, or at least their perception of reality, will also be positive. In contrast, when a person has a negative mindset, then their perception of reality becomes negative, resulting in depression, anxiety, and a greater tendency toward procrastination. While this might appear to be a fixed situation, and one that cannot be changed in any significant way, the truth of the matter is that a person's mindset can virtually be programmed in any direction, positive or negative. This chapter will explore the impact thoughts have on procrastination, as well as the methods for changing those thoughts, thereby creating a mindset that avoids procrastination altogether.

The Chemistry of Success/Failure

When you think of the human brain, you probably think of a solid, gray mass that resides in your head. While this is true to a degree, the fact is that the brain is far more complex than it appears. Rather than just being a large lump of gray matter, your brain is a bio-electric computer of sorts. Electrical impulses are constantly firing throughout your brain, sending everything—including signals, thoughts, memories, feelings, and even desires—throughout your body and mind. The problem is that most people believe that the state of their brain is relatively fixed, in that how they think, feel, or perceive reality is unchangeable, much like the color of their eyes or the number of fingers they have. However, the reality is that the brain can be literally programmed, much the way any computer or computerized device can be programmed. All it takes is a little understanding of how the brain works and a little effort to change its current way of thinking.

The first thing to understand is how repetition affects your very mindset. Neuroscience has shown that the brain contains synapses: these synapses are like fingers that fire out electrical impulses that release chemicals into the body. A good way to envision this is to take your hands and place your fingers together. Then move your fingers apart a couple of inches, maintaining their alignment. The synapses in your brain don't actually touch, instead they face each other, like your fingers, and shoot electrical impulses across space in between, space known as the "synaptic cleft." When one synapse fires an electrical impulse into the other, the receiving synapse sends that impulse to a part of the brain that creates a chemical reaction. This is how positive thoughts create positive feelings, and negative thoughts create negative feelings.

What most people don't know is the fact that since the synapses aren't connected, they can be realigned. This means that the alignment that allows for negativity can be changed, creating an alignment that allows for positivity. Known as "neuroplasticity," this is the malleable condition of the brain. Therefore, rather than being a victim of your thoughts and feelings, you can actually rewrite how your brain works, changing the very nature of your thoughts and feelings in the process. Needless to say, this process is a gradual one, requiring a great deal of effort and time. However, just like lifting weights, if you put in the time and effort, the results will follow. The trick is to tweak your thoughts from those of a negative mindset to those of a positive mindset; one filled with hope, optimism, and inspiration.

The final thing to understand is why it seems as though your particular mindset is natural. In addition to forming alignments, synapses can also move closer together over time. Although they will never touch, the distance an electrical impulse has to cover—moving from one synapse to another—can shrink over time. This is due to repetition. The more you think a particular thought, the easier that thought becomes. Therefore, if you constantly think about failure, the synapses responsible for that thought and the fear that accompanies it will move closer and closer together, making those thoughts more readily available. However, this applies to a positive mindset, as well. Once you successfully reprogram your mind, you will create the neurological pathways that allow you to have positive thoughts and feelings quickly and easily. In a way, it's a bit like programming shortcuts to sites on the Internet. Rather than having to take the time to navigate to a site, you simply push one button, and you are there. This is how thoughts work in the brain. Once you create those shortcuts, you make that way of thinking easy and natural.

Change Your Perspective

The reason this is important is that the nature of your mindset will directly affect your decision-making process. Needless to say, a big part of that process is deciding when to address the tasks and projects at hand. If you have a negative mindset, you will be far more likely to procrastinate than if your mindset is positive in nature. Therefore, being able to reprogram your mind is essential if you want to be able to change your habits in a significant and lasting way. In short, the best way to change your behaviors is to change your perspective. Once you change your perspective, your habits and behaviors will change largely on their own, requiring very little effort on your part.

The first step to changing your perspective is to change the alignment of your synapses. While this sounds like something only a neurosurgeon can do, the fact is that anyone can accomplish this goal. The trick is to begin thinking in a different direction. For example, if you find that you constantly focus on the likelihood of failing at any task you perform, start imagining yourself succeeding instead. Take the time to replace the vision of falling short with one of being successful. Picture yourself handing in the project on time, or even better, ahead of schedule. Instead of imagining your boss ridiculing you for inferior work, picture them praising you for a job well done. Create the reality you wish to experience, not the one you are afraid of, or the one you remember from past situations. This is how you change the formation of your synapses, causing you to create a positive mindset in which hope, optimism, and self-confidence begin to replace the fear of failure and low self-esteem that caused you to procrastinate in the first place.

The second step to changing your perspective is to change the distance of the synapses. As mentioned before, the closer the synapses are, the easier the thought processes become. The trick here is to create repetition. If you only think positive thoughts from time to time, the synapses will remain further apart, allowing them to realign more easily back into their previous, negative alignment. However, if you take the time and effort to think positive thoughts all through the day, you will shrink the synaptic cleft, making your positive mindset easier to access and easier to maintain. A good way to achieve this goal is to create a list of five positive questions that you ask yourself at least three times a day. You can choose to ask these questions first thing in the morning, when you are having lunch, and last thing at night. Adding more times during the day will only increase your results, giving you faster and more significant success. A good set of questions to ask include the following:

- What can I be grateful for today?

- What will bring me happiness today?

- How can I flirt with someone I am interested in today?

- How is today better than yesterday?

- What can I do to be my best self today?

When you ask these questions, you begin to shift your focus from any negative thoughts to more positive, upbeat thoughts. This will help to create a positive mindset, one that brings happiness, confidence, and purpose to your day-to-day life. The more you ask these questions, the more you will change the way your brain functions. In as little as thirty days, your mindset will have been altered significantly. Another thirty days will see your mindset established, making your newly created positivity the new way you think each and every day.

Another way to change your way of thinking is to change your perspective on who you are. This can be done much the same way as changing your thoughts. In this case, you will write down three words that describe your ideal self, the person you ultimately want to be. These three words can be anything at all, and they can change over time as you begin to move forward in the direction of self-improvement. The trick is to repeat these words all throughout the day, making them the mantra of your improved self. Words such as exciting, happy, optimistic, gracious, confident, charming, commanding, inspiring, determined, and the like, can form your mantra. The important thing is to choose words that strike a chord, words that inspire you to be your best. Once you have your words, repeat them as often as you can, including when you wake up, when you go to bed, and all throughout the day. You can recite them when driving to work, standing in line at the grocery store, or even riding an elevator. The more you recite your words, the more your mind will identify with them, changing your sense of self, transforming you into the person you most want to be.

Change the Vernacular

The previous sections have focused on how to change your mindset, thereby changing how you think and how you perceive yourself. By replacing a negative mindset full of fear, dread, and self-loathing with a positive mindset full of hope, excitement, and confidence, you can remove the very causes of procrastination from within. The result is that your behaviors and habits will change automatically, giving you all the tools you need to achieve the success you have always dreamed of. However, there is another way in which you can change your perspective on things, one that reprograms your mind by changing the very definition of the tasks or projects at hand. This is the process of "changing the vernacular."

Many examples of this process can be seen in day-to-day life, especially in terms of specific jobs and their descriptions. At one time, a person who collected trash was known as a garbage man, whereas today, they are referred to as a "sanitation engineer." Maids are now known as housekeepers or domestic assistants. Secretaries are now personal assistants. Janitors are now custodians, and the list goes on and on. The reason for these title changes was to improve the image of the job at hand. Title changes resulted in a higher sense of self-esteem within those performing the jobs, as well as an increased number of people applying to fill the needed positions. In the end, even though the job itself didn't change by changing the title, it took on a more positive sounding tone. This is precisely how you can change your perspective on the tasks and projects you face each and every day.

More often than not, the things you procrastinate on are those things you dread doing. For example, if you hate washing dishes, then you will put off washing dishes for as long as you can. The very sound of those words will be enough to make you shudder and find any excuse to avoid facing the task. However, by changing the name of the task, you can change the very tone of it as well. Instead of calling the task "washing dishes," you can call it "preparing to make dinner," or "beautifying the kitchen." Although the task itself hasn't changed, if you focus on a different element, such as the desired result, or another task that is more pleasant, then you become less likely to procrastinate as your motivation is increased. Everyone likes to eat dinner, and everyone enjoys a beautiful kitchen. Therefore, focusing on those elements can be enough to change your perspective completely, removing the desire to procrastinate as a result.

This can be done for even the most fear-inspiring tasks as well. Public speaking, for example, is something that most people dread, and thus they put off for as long as possible, reducing their chances of success in the process. The trick is to change your perception of the event by changing the event's name. Rather than calling it "public speaking" call it "impressing my boss," or "impressing the person I have a crush on." This takes the focus from the task and places it on a desirable outcome; one that might not even have anything to do with the task itself, such as in the case of impressing someone you have a crush on. Once you create this expectation, you shift how your mind perceives the task, giving you the incentive and optimism to face it head-on without delay.

Negativity as a Positive

One final thing to consider is that negative thoughts aren't always bad in and of themselves. The simple truth is that everyone has negative thoughts each and every day. This is due to the fact that the human brain is hard-wired to predict danger, thereby protecting the individual from as much harm as possible. Subsequently, having negative thoughts isn't the real problem. Rather, the problem is when you allow those thoughts to control your emotions and actions. The thoughts themselves can actually serve as a tool for success when you know how to use them correctly.

The first thing to do is to become aware of your negative thoughts. More often than not, people either try to suppress any negative thoughts that come their way, or they allow them to play in the background, like a radio constantly playing music that undermines self-confidence and self-esteem. However, when you take the time to recognize those thoughts and ask why they are there, you might just get some insights that will prove useful in the end. If, for example, you are afraid of failing at a task or project because you failed a similar task or project in the past, take the time to contemplate the reasons for your past failure. This will enable you to learn valuable lessons, ones that can keep you from making the same mistakes as before, thereby increasing your chances of success.

A good way to turn negative thoughts into tools for success is to create a checklist from them. If, for example, you are afraid of giving a speech in public, and the fear stems from the fact that your last public speaking event was a disaster, take the time to list out what went wrong the last time around. If you forgot your lines, write that down. If you experienced difficulty in speaking because your mouth dried up, write that down. If you tripped over your shoelaces, or the batteries in your laser pointer died, write that down. Carefully dissect the things that went wrong before and then create a checklist for your next event. This list will include such things as follows:

- Put fresh batteries in your laser pointer and have extras on hand.

- Drink water before your speech and have a glass of water on hand.

- Don't wear shoes with laces.

- Keep bullet points of your speech in view in case you get distracted.

Now, rather than simply suppressing your fear, you turn it into a helpful aid, one that ensures you are fully prepared for your next endeavor and that you will avoid the pitfalls that robbed you of success the last time around. Furthermore, tell yourself that success is the default result and that only a lack of preparation will keep you from achieving it. Now that you are better prepared, you can expect a better performance, one that will put the painful memories to rest and replace the negative perspective with a positive one. This is how you use your inherent fears to your advantage.

Chapter 6: Ten Proven Ways to Beat Laziness

Laziness is probably the hardest cause of procrastination to overcome. This is because it is more than a mere bad habit or behavior that needs to be changed. In essence, laziness is a personality trait, something that affects not only behavior but a person's outlook on life in general. Therefore, it usually takes more than a few tweaks to change behavior caused by laziness. Fortunately, there are several techniques that will enable a person to begin to address their lazy tendencies and create a more productive, positive mindset instead. This chapter will focus on ten such techniques, each proven to effectively address specific causes and symptoms of laziness. By implementing all or even just a few of the methods discussed in this chapter, even the "laziest" person can begin to affect meaningful and lasting change in their life.

Be Forgiving

One of the most important steps to overcoming laziness is to be forgiving. The simple truth is that laziness can be a vicious cycle, one started by a lazy thought or intention but perpetuated by guilt, depression, and a general feeling of low self-worth. More often than not, this impacts people who are aware of their laziness and want to overcome it. After all, those who are completely lazy and have no interest in changing their ways have no reason to feel guilty. However, when a person seeks to improve themselves but falls back into lazy habits, they can create a vicious cycle that keeps them from ever breaking free.

The only way to break out of such a cycle is to end the mindset of guilt. Rather than allowing guilt and regret to fill your mind, you need to be forgiving of yourself. Take the time to recognize that you are facing a significant struggle and that setbacks will happen. Give yourself permission to both let go of past mistakes and not take future mistakes to heart. Understand that the process will take time, but that as long as you stay in the race, eventually you will cross the finish line and create the change you are so desperate for. Any time you feel yourself slipping back into guilt and frustration, remember that you are not alone and that plenty of others struggle with the same issues you face. Therefore, you are not a bad person; rather, you are a good person who is simply trying to break bad habits.

Take the First Step

When it comes to addressing laziness on a day-to-day basis, few methods are as effective as taking the first step. This comes down to a matter of physics: creating momentum. Anyone familiar with physics knows that it takes the greatest amount of energy to set a still object into motion. Once that object is moving, it takes less energy to keep it moving. In fact, this is the first Law of Motion discovered by Isaac Newton. Simply put, when an object is at rest or in motion, it will remain so unless acted upon by another force. Thus, the hardest part is to go from still to moving. Once you get the proverbial ball rolling, everything suddenly becomes easier.

How this translates into productivity is quite simple. As long as you don't take the first step, the project or task at hand will remain at its most difficult level. However, once you take the first step, you set things into motion. Once in motion, it becomes easier to keep working than to stop, just as it was easier to stay still than to get moving. Therefore, all you need to do to overcome laziness when facing any task or project is to take that all-important first step. After that, each and every subsequent step becomes effortless, resulting in you achieving your goal before you realize it.

Begin Early

A big mistake many people make when it comes to addressing work of any kind is to leave it until later, for a time when they might feel more energized or motivated. The bottom line is that the longer you wait to start a task or project, the harder it becomes to ever get started. This is another example of the Law of Motion at work. Once you start delaying work, it becomes easier to keep delaying it. The more time that goes by, the more effort it takes to actually stop procrastinating and begin tackling the task at hand.

Needless to say, the best way to overcome this pitfall is to always begin working early. By starting right away, you avoid getting into the rut of putting work off for later. This actually makes it easier to get started, as you don't have any negative momentum to contend with. Instead, you only have to put in as much effort as it takes to get the ball rolling, then the rest will take care of itself. The fact of the matter is that everyone begins early; the only question is what direction they choose to go. Many choose to begin procrastinating, which makes their day harder as a result. Alternatively, those who begin working ensure that their day gets easier as it unfolds, removing the stress and fatigue that lead to further procrastination.

Take Plenty of Breaks

In the fast-paced environment of these modern times, a commonly held belief is that in order to be productive, you must always be working. Any time spent on anything, except work, is seen as time wasted. This is why lunch "hours" have been reduced to thirty-minutes in many cases, and shorter breaks have become all but non-existent in most workplace environments. However, instead of increasing productivity, a lack of downtime actually undermines a person's performance, resulting in less productivity and lower quality results. This is because a lack of downtime leads to the average person becoming burned out and thus ineffective at the task they are performing.

In order to avoid this situation, it is vital that you take plenty of breaks throughout the day. For some people, this might mean ten minutes every hour, whereas, for others, it might mean thirty minutes every couple of hours. The important thing is to find what works best for you and begin creating your schedule around that. Although it might seem counterintuitive to work less in order to get more done, the simple truth is that when your energy levels are restored, and your mind is refreshed, you perform at peak efficiency, making your efforts go further than if you are tired and overwhelmed. Too many people taking these breaks might appear to be lazy in nature; however, they actually help to prevent the lazy tendencies that come from fatigue, stress, and a general state of burnout as the result of working too hard for too long.

Eliminate Distractions

Laziness can have many different faces, making it hard to recognize at times, as it can appear to be something altogether different. A good example of this is the type of laziness that encourages a person to choose the more fun option rather than getting to work on the harder, more demanding tasks at hand. The problem here is that in an age of social media, cell phones, and constant access to the Internet, it can be all too easy to find things to do that are infinitely more fun than the work that needs to get done. A few minutes here and there can add up quickly, resulting in a day's productivity lost to an endless stream of distractions.

The best way to overcome this form of laziness is to eliminate distractions whenever possible. While turning off your cell phone may not be an option, especially if you receive work calls on your phone, or you use your phone for emergencies with loved ones, turning off notifications or even Internet access can make all the difference. Overall, the more distractions you eliminate, the fewer temptations you will face throughout the day, making it easier to stay focused on your work. Not only will this make you more productive, but it will also reduce errors made due to a lack of concentration.

Keep Your Motivation Refreshed

As already discussed, one of the main issues with laziness is that a truly lazy person sees work as a painful process. This means that instead of seeing a challenge or a chance to achieve success, they see hardship and drudgery, things that hardly inspire motivation. Since work has all the appearances of being painful and meaningless, it can be all too easy to avoid it at all costs. Fortunately, there is an easy trick, one that doesn't necessarily change the nature of work; rather, it shifts the focus of the individual in such a way as to keep their motivation refreshed. This is the trick of contemplating the downsides and upsides for achieving the task at hand.

For example, if you need to accomplish a difficult task before you are able to go home for the day, rather than focusing on the size and complexity of the project, you should focus on the reward of getting to go home once it is done. The longer it takes to accomplish, the longer you are stuck at work. Suddenly, instead of being painful, tackling the task at hand becomes desirable, as it directly relates to your ability to go home, put your feet up, and be as lazy as you want. Every task or project will have a reward associated with its completion, offering a way to keep your motivation refreshed no matter the situation.

Declutter Your Life

Another common cause of laziness is the sense of being constantly overwhelmed. This is usually the case when a person either has too many things to do at any given time or when their schedule isn't as organized as it should be. In either case, the simple solution to this scenario is to declutter your life. Just as you would declutter a workspace by getting rid of junk and unnecessary items, so too can you declutter your schedule by getting rid of unnecessary tasks and organizing what remains. Once you declutter your life, you will be less intimidated by the tasks and errands you need to do each day, enabling you to face your day with greater confidence and energy.

A good way to remove the unnecessary items from your daily to-do list is to sit down and ask which tasks are absolutely essential. Ask yourself if you only had a couple of hours to get things done, which things would you choose. When you know which items aren't important, you can remove them from your list, freeing up some time and energy and thus decluttering your schedule. While some of the things you remove might be able to be eliminated altogether, others might still have to be addressed. In this case, you can simply place them on another day, the way you would put unnecessary items elsewhere in order to clean up your workspace. Once your day is less overwhelming, you won't be so tempted to avoid it, thus eliminating the allure of lazy behavior.

Accept Setbacks

Any time you fear failure, it can be all too tempting to avoid tackling the harder, more daunting tasks, choosing instead to stick with easier tasks or no tasks at all. This goes back to the understanding that laziness is the result of a negative association with work, thus causing a person to avoid work at all costs. Therefore, the stronger your fear of failure, the more likely you are to become lazy in order to avoid facing your fears.

Needless to say, failure is something that cannot be avoided completely, no matter how hard a person tries. Instead, setbacks will come in many shapes and sizes. The trick here is to accept this fact and let go of the need to avoid failure in the first place. The bottom line is that even the best, most successful people experience failure in their lives. That said, failure is not anything to be ashamed of or to fear. After all, despite their failures, such people remain highly successful. Therefore, the only way forward is to let yourself off the hook when it comes to setbacks. You will face them from time to time, but they won't defeat you, nor will they define you. Instead, they will teach you valuable lessons that will enable you to become better and stronger. Once you realize this, you will be able to tackle any task or project, no longer worrying about the outcome.

Surround Yourself with Positive Energy

Whenever you spend time with a person, one thing you realize is that the energy of that person tends to affect your own energy. In other words, if you spend time with someone who is hyper and agitated, you will become agitated as well. The same holds true for depressed, uninspired people. When you spend time with anyone who has low motivation or who is lazy, you will begin to feel the same, regardless of your true nature. This becomes even more real in the event that you spend time in a crowd of people of the same mindset. Therefore, one sure way to overcome laziness is to stay as far away from lazy, low energy people as you can, surrounding yourself with positive, highly motivated people instead.

When you surround yourself with positive energy, that energy will begin to affect you the same way that negative or agitated energy will. This means that you will start to feel highly motivated, optimistic, and even eager to tackle any task or project you need to accomplish. Furthermore, by surrounding yourself with such people, you will create a support group. A support group provides constant encouragement that will enable you to be your best at all times. Any time you find yourself slipping back into bad habits or struggling to overcome lazy tendencies, the best thing to do is to find highly motivated people to spend time with, so that you can recharge your energy and restore your sense of inspiration.

Embrace Laziness

The final trick to overcoming laziness is to actually embrace laziness. This doesn't mean that you should be lazy all day, every day. Instead, it means that if you truly believe that you are lazy, then be as lazy as you want to be when the time is right. One of the problems that most people face when they try to overcome laziness is that they try to deny themselves the pleasure of being lazy altogether. Unfortunately, when you deprive yourself of something, it can cause you to desire it even more. Thus, if you try to be productive at all times, including on your days off and in your downtime, you might actually set yourself up for wanting to be lazier at work than ever before.

To avoid this pitfall, the trick is to put all your effort into doing the right thing at the right time. Thus, when you are at work, be as productive as possible, avoiding lazy behavior completely; however, once you get home and kick your shoes off, become completely lazy, getting your fill of downtime, rest, and general non-productivity. When you allow yourself to be totally lazy during your downtime, you won't need to get your fill when there is work to be done. In a way, it's just like sleep. When you get enough sleep at night, you don't feel tired during the day. Alternatively, if you are sleep-deprived, you struggle to stay awake during the day, since your body craves the sleep it lacks. This is how your mind works as well, craving what it lacks, even when the time isn't right. Therefore, by letting yourself be totally lazy when the time is right, you will be more productive when it's time to get to work.

Chapter 7: Plan it Out: Six Steps to Getting Things Done

For the past few decades, cookbooks have been one of the most successful niches in publishing. More and more cookbooks sell each year, creating a very profitable career for anyone with culinary skills. Although new and exciting recipes are the main reason for the constant sale of cookbooks, another commonly overlooked reason is the directions that go with those recipes. If the average person had to guess at how to make a meal, they would wind up making countless errors before figuring it out. Fortunately, the directions provided in cookbooks take out the guesswork, ensuring the person following the recipe gets the best results each and every time. This same approach can be used to eliminate the struggle and guesswork when it comes to doing anything in life, not just making dinner. When you come up with a clear, concise plan, you can ensure that your to-do list gets done completely and effectively each and every time, without the need to reinvent the wheel day in and day out. This chapter will discuss the value of planning things out, and how sticking to a well thought out plan can make all the difference when it comes to not only getting things done, but getting things done right.

Set SMART Goals

The first step to creating a plan is to establish the goal you want to achieve. Unfortunately, this step is usually the one most people rush through, if they even pay attention to it at all. The end result is that their efforts are scattered and ineffective, undermining their chances of success in a real and significant way. In order to maximize your chances of successfully achieving your goals, it is critical that you learn to set SMART goals; ones that structure your direction, effort, and time. The following steps will help you to set SMART goals in your life:

- Specific: whenever you set a goal, you need to make sure it is specific in every way. Simply saying you want to write a book, for example, is far too vague a goal to achieve. The trick here would be to decide the exact book you want to write, including the type of book, the word count, and even the title.

- Measurable: the next step to creating a SMART goal is to make the progress measurable. This breaks down all the necessary parts of the goal, turning the big project into smaller tasks. You might choose to set milestones for writing a set number of words per day or per week, establishing a momentum of sorts. As you check off each milestone, you can track your progress to the overall result you are striving for, namely writing your book.

- Attainable: while being clear and specific regarding your goals is critical, it is also very important to be realistic. If you are spread too thin with the responsibilities you currently have, or you aren't a very good writer, then you might need to rethink your decision. Therefore, always be sure that the goal you set for yourself is one that is achievable. This doesn't mean it has to be easy; rather, it simply means that it has to be possible.

- Relevant: another element to creating a SMART goal is the relevance of the goal itself. If you don't really want to write a book, there is no point in setting the goal as you won't care about accomplishing it. Therefore, you need to make sure that the goal you set is one that is inspiring and meaningful to you. This will help to keep you motivated, especially in the most difficult times.

- Time-bound: this is when you set a specific timeframe within which you want to write your book. Without that timeframe, you give yourself the opportunity to procrastinate indefinitely, putting off your dream until the "right time" comes. Therefore, in addition to choosing the goal you want, you will add that you want to get your book written by the end of the year. Furthermore, you need to add the time you will start putting your plan into motion, including timeframes within which to accomplish the specific milestones of your overall plan. This makes you more accountable in terms of time, thereby reducing the likelihood of procrastination.

Create the Right Environment

Once you have created a SMART goal for yourself, the next step is to create the right environment for accomplishing that goal. Simply putting in the time and effort isn't always enough to ensure that the job gets done. Instead, it is vital that you create the right environment, one that is designed to help you achieve your goal. After all, if you try to write your book while sitting on the sofa watching TV, the chances are you won't get much further than the title page. Therefore, once you decide on a goal, it is essential that you create an environment that will help you to focus on the task at hand, thereby giving you the best chance for success.

First and foremost, you need to eliminate any and all distractions. Removing distractions will help you to stay focused on the task at hand, which will increase your efficiency as well as the quality of your work. Additionally, a clean, organized environment has been proven to go a long way to reducing stress, increasing inspiration, and making any task more enjoyable overall. Therefore, take the time to create a space that is inviting, organized, and distraction-free. This will help you to get into the right frame of mind for getting any task or project done, no matter how large it might be.

Another way that you can create a better working environment is to play music in the background. Needless to say, different styles of music will create different mindsets, so it is important to find the one that suits your mood at the time, as well as one that helps you to focus and get your work done. While silence can prove good for some people, most people struggle to keep their minds focused on silent conditions. The end result is that their mind wanders, contemplating everything but the task at hand. When you play music in the background, it can have the effect of soothing your mind, thereby keeping it from being restless and wandering in every direction.

Another way to get your mind to focus on the task at hand is to meditate before you begin work. By taking as little as five minutes to sit and actively clear your mind, you can create a mindset that will be more focused on the present. Getting rid of the clutter and chaos in your mind is as important as getting rid of the clutter and chaos in your physical environment. In a way, this is the process of creating the right mental environment, one that helps you to be productive and efficient, thereby enabling you to accomplish all of your goals.

Set Some Easy Rules

As already mentioned, chaos plays a big role when it comes to procrastination. The more chaotic your environment, schedule, and mindset, the more likely you are to put things off, thereby reducing your chances of accomplishing your goals. Fortunately, if you create a few simple rules that you follow each and every day, not only can you eliminate most of the chaos from your life, you can prevent it from ever coming back. This will go a long way toward overcoming procrastination once and for all.

One easy rule to follow is what is known as the Two-Minute Rule. This simply means that any task that can be accomplished in two minutes or less should be addressed immediately. Although this may seem counterintuitive, especially with regard to focusing on one task at a time and avoiding distractions, the bottom line is that it will take as much time to write down or reschedule a two-minute task as it would to actually complete it. Therefore, rather than wasting extra time, or allowing those small tasks to add up, simply knock them out as they arise. This will keep your schedule free of clutter, thereby enabling you to stay on track when it comes to the larger tasks and projects.

Another easy, yet effective rule, is to write down any ideas as they come into your mind. Sometimes you might have an inspired thought as you are working on something, but rather than writing it down, you tuck it away in the back of your mind. This has the effect of splitting your attention. Now, instead of being wholly focused on the task at hand, you are also focused on remembering that important piece of information. The more ideas you tuck away in your mind, the more cluttered your mind becomes. In order to avoid this, always take the time to write random ideas down. This will keep your mind clear and focused, while also ensuring that you don't forget what might turn out to be a real breakthrough later on.

The final rule to apply to your day-to-day life is to keep your goals simple. For example, if you want to begin organizing your day each morning, rather than setting your alarm an hour earlier and forcing yourself to write a full itinerary, simply start with taking five minutes in the morning to write a shortlist of four or five things you want to accomplish. As you master the art of making your daily list you can move on to the next step, which might be spending five or ten minutes creating a schedule for the day. Once you master that step, you can add another, and so on. Instead of jumping into the proverbial deep end, take it gradually, one step at a time, keeping the goals simple, achievable, and fun.

Maintain Your Energy Levels

The importance of maintaining your energy levels cannot be overstated when it comes to accomplishing goals and achieving success in your day-to-day life. Unfortunately, this step is the one that most people skip over in order to scavenge time for other steps. The end result is that even though they might be doing everything else right, when their energy levels aren't at their highest, their results won't be as good as they might be otherwise. Therefore, it is absolutely essential that you keep your energy levels as high as possible at all times.

One way to do this is to take care of your body. Ensure that you get the right amount of sleep each and every night and that your sleep is of the right quality. Invest in a good mattress, make sure your room is totally dark, and eliminate as much noise as possible to create an environment where you will get good, restful sleep, which will recharge your batteries.

Another critical element when keeping your energy levels high is to eat right. Avoid foods heavy with sugar, salt, or fat, as these will only serve to drain your energy, not restore it. Instead, eat foods rich in vitamins, minerals, and protein, such as eggs, vegetables, beans, and fish. Even though it might take more time to make and eat a proper breakfast, the energy you get from that breakfast will make you far more productive all day long. In the end, your productivity will increase, despite the investment of time.

Avoiding burnout is another proven way to maintain your energy levels all throughout the day. The best way to achieve this goal is to schedule regular breaks throughout the day, ensuring you don't get bogged down in a task or project, which will drain you of your physical and mental energy. A good brisk walk for five minutes can make all the difference, getting your blood flowing, and raising your respiratory rate. Not only will this reinvigorate your body, but it will also help to clear and refresh your mind.

Set Yourself Up for Success

The next step that will help you to get things done each and every day is to set yourself up for success. This has a few aspects to it, each with its own impact on your ability to stay focused and to get things done. The first aspect is to create a daily plan. Many people choose to do this first thing in the morning as they are getting ready for work. While this may work for some, the fact is that the best time to create such a plan is actually the night before. This is because you can use your downtime at the end of the day to come up with the goals you want to achieve the next day, rather than forcing yourself to think in such specific terms right when you wake up. Take the time to list out the things you want to accomplish, as well as the desired timeframe. In short, write out a basic itinerary, one that will organize your day and keep you on track to accomplishing your goals.

Another aspect of this step is to reflect on your progress on a regular basis. When you simply put in the effort without taking the time to review how effective that effort is, you can get stuck in a rut, one that might not even help you to accomplish your goals. However, when you take the time to review your progress, including your successes and setbacks, then you can discover what efforts are beneficial and what efforts need to be replaced. The best time to do this is at the end of the day, when you can reflect on the events of the day and determine where you stand regarding the goals you want to achieve. In fact, this can segue into creating your itinerary for the next day, as you can determine the improvements and changes you need to make in real-time.

Find What Works for You

The final step that will help you to achieve your goals is to find what works for you. A big problem that many people face when trying to improve their lives is that they assume that what works for one person will work for them. Although all of the methods and techniques covered in this book are proven to be effective, the bottom line is that not all of them might be effective for you. Therefore, it is critical that you try each and every one in order to know which are useful and which just don't work for you.

A good example of this is with reviewing your day and creating an itinerary. As already mentioned, the ideal time to complete these tasks is at the end of the day. However, that might not actually be right for you. Instead, you might find that first thing in the morning is the best time for you. Perhaps you need to sleep on things in order to sort them out in your mind, finding meaning and answers that otherwise wouldn't be available. Or you might find that setting aside time in the middle of the day is best for you. In the end, it doesn't matter when you perform these tasks, what matters is that you use the tools that work for you in the best way possible.

Another example is meditation. Many people practice meditation in order to clear their minds, helping them to be calm and more focused. While this method is effective, it might not be right for everyone. If you are a highly energetic person, meditation might actually agitate you rather than calming and clearing your mind. In this case, you might need to engage in more energetic activity, such as kickboxing, running, or some similar exercise. This would help you to burn off excess energy, thereby relaxing you and clearing your mind. Thus, even though kickboxing and meditation seem completely different, they can, in fact, achieve the same goal. Therefore, the trick is to understand the fundamentals of self-improvement and discover the methods that help you to achieve them in your own life.

Chapter 8: How to Get Started on Any Project NOW

The analogy of momentum has already been discussed with regard to beating procrastination. Simply put, the hardest step in any journey is the first step. Once that all-important first step is taken, all the others tend to fall into place, requiring less and less effort as the momentum builds. That said, few things are as important to overcoming procrastination than finding the motivation and energy to get the ball rolling on any project or task. Fortunately, there are several tips and tricks that can help even the worst procrastinator to get started on the task at hand, thereby enabling them to accomplish anything they set their mind to. This chapter will discuss several of those tips and tricks, approaching the subject from all sides, including emotional, organizational, and social. By the time you finish reading this chapter, you will have all the tools you need to get started on any project *now*.

Get Excited

Few things make as much of a difference when it comes to productivity as excitement. The more excited you are about something, the more energy and enthusiasm you will have for getting that thing done. This can be seen each and every year when countless children all around the world wake up at the crack of dawn on Christmas morning. Compare that to the countless times the average child struggles to get out of bed on a school day, or on any day when chores, doctor's visits, and the like await them. The simple lesson here is that the average child isn't lazy or sleep-deprived, rather they are simply unmotivated when it comes to facing the days of drudgery. Alternatively, when an exciting day awaits, their energy levels soar through the roof. This phenomenon isn't restricted to young people; instead, it affects the hearts and minds of people of all ages.

With this in mind, the trick to getting started on something is to get excited about it. In a way, you need to treat the task or project like Christmas Day itself, promising all sorts of rewards and prizes. One of the best ways to achieve this goal is to create what is called a "vision board." Vision boards can be any kind of board, including a corkboard, dry erase board, or even a piece of poster board. The purpose of the board is to create a space where you can put all of the things that provide inspiration for your task or project. For example, if you need to paint your house and you are struggling to find the motivation, get a piece of poster board and fill it with pictures of painted rooms similar to the vision you have of how yours will look when it's done. The more you remind yourself of how wonderful the finished product will be, the more inspired you will be to get to work on making it happen.

More often than not, vision boards are used for long term projects or goals, things that will change your life in a real and significant way. An example of this would be losing weight. Perhaps you have struggled to start an exercise and diet regimen, keeping you from achieving your ambition of creating a healthier, slimmer you. Putting images of people you aspire to look like on a vision board will help you to keep your eyes on the proverbial prize, helping you to not only get started, but to also keep going even when times get tough. In addition to photos, you can put inspirational quotes, specific goals to keep you on track, and even images to track your progress, thus helping you to appreciate how well you are doing at all times. In the end, the most important thing is that the items on your vision board keep you motivated and excited, thereby encouraging you to put in the effort that will eventually allow you to achieve your goal and bask in the rewards that await.

Write it Down

Another proven way to help you get started on any task or project is to actually write your task or project down. Although this may not sound like much, it can actually make all the difference. The simple fact is that until you write down a goal, it remains nothing more than a pipedream, a fantasy that only exists in your mind. As a result, it never takes on any real form, making it easier to ignore, or even worse, forget about altogether. However, once you take that all-important step of putting your ideas down on paper, you take the fantasy and give it form, thereby giving it a reality. Now, instead of being just a dream, it becomes a vision, a goal, something your mind can now treat seriously because your eyes can see it in front of you.

Creating this visual quite literally shifts where your dream exists in your mind. As long as your dream remains a pure fantasy, it resides in your imagination. However, once you write down your dream, it becomes a problem to solve, thereby moving from your imagination to your intellect. Now your brain can start working on how to accomplish your goal, rather than using the image as an escape from reality. The important thing is to take the time to write out your dream in as much detail as possible, even listing all of the fears and concerns you have about turning that dream into reality. By putting everything down on paper, you literally jump-start your mind to figure out the solutions to all of those problems, thereby giving you the answers you need to get started on achieving that particular goal.

Needless to say, you don't want to write down your task or project in a way that focuses solely on the obstacles and challenges it presents. Although listing those things will help you to start solving them in your mind, the important thing is to also keep a positive spin on things, making sure you write down all the rewards of a successful outcome. Additionally, you can write down all of the negatives that would result from you not starting your project, providing the stick as well as the carrot when it comes to motivation. The simple truth of the matter is that such negative motivations can prove more influential than positive ones. Thus, they should be used to keep you inspired and motivated at all times. For example, if you want to look for a new job, you can use staying in your current job as negative motivation. List a few of the worst aspects of your job as a consequence of not working on achieving your goal and getting that better job. Furthermore, it is vital that you refer to this written goal as often as possible, at least a few times a day. This will keep it real in your mind and will keep you motivated to do whatever it takes to turn your dream into reality, thereby improving your life and achieving the happiness you deserve.

Commit Time to Your Project

One of the most common words used by the most successful people to explain how they achieve their success is: "commitment." No matter what the task or project might be, until you commit yourself to it, you will never put in the effort needed to accomplish your goal, and thus achieve the success you crave. The first element that you need to commit in order to get started on your task or project is time. After all, no amount of resources, inspiration, or energy will be of any use if you don't have the time needed to accomplish your goal. Therefore, before you try to find the tools and resources you need for your task or project, you must first set aside specific time to work on turning your goal into reality.

Unfortunately, this is where most people go wrong when it comes to starting a task or project, specifically a large one. More often than not, they wait until they have enough time to accomplish the entire task at once. Therefore, they only commit the time to the task when they have a large amount of time to spare. The trick is not to wait until you have large amounts of time. Instead, you should devote small portions of time to get started on the project. As little as fifteen minutes a day can be all that it takes to do any research on your project, acquire necessary resources, or even begin tackling the project in small doses. Thus, instead of waiting until you have enough time to do everything, simply set aside some of the time you do have in order to get as much done as you can.

The main side effect of this method is that it creates momentum. As you start working on your task or project, even for just fifteen minutes, suddenly, you crave more time so that you can get more done. The next thing you know, you are rearranging your schedule in order to find more time for the project that you had been procrastinating on for ages. Even if you can't find more time than the fifteen minutes a day, the bottom line is that those small doses will add up, as will the results of your efforts. After a couple of weeks, you will have spent a couple of hours on your project. That amount of time will put a huge dent into the overall process, giving you a head start at the very least. More often than not, those results add up sooner than you realize, seeing you accomplish your goal without ever having had to face it all at once. Therefore, no matter how little time you might have available, when you set aside a small amount of time each and every day, you will be able to achieve any task or project, no matter how large or complex.

Commit Resources to Your Project

Once you commit time to your task or project, the next step is to commit resources to it as well. This is another way that you take your dream and give it relevance in the material world. The simple act of purchasing the right equipment necessary to achieve your goal can make all the difference when it comes to taking the first step to getting that goal accomplished. A good example of this is with starting an exercise regimen. If you want to start running each and every day, once you set aside the time necessary for your run, the next step would be to acquire a good pair of running shoes and some comfortable athletic wear to go with them. The act of purchasing these items is an act of committing to the process, thereby making it more real in your mind. Being able to see and feel your running shoes makes your goal tangible, and that is all-important when it comes to getting started.

Sometimes a task or project may not need equipment as such, making this step appear more challenging as a result. The good thing is that no matter what the task or project is, it will always need resources of one form or another. For example, if you want to write a book, you might not need any extra equipment, especially if you already have a computer or laptop that you will use for your writing. In this case, you could create folders on your computer for finished documents. Additionally, you might set aside specific space within which to work. Creating space is a way of giving your goal life in the real world, especially if you don't use that space for anything else. Therefore, no matter how little your task or project requires in terms of resources, there will always be something you can do to bring your dream into the physical world, thereby making it more real and thus more necessary to get started on.

Another resource that almost all tasks and projects require is cold, hard cash. This is another way that you can commit resources and thus stop procrastinating once and for all. Although setting aside money in a savings account is a good option for a more expensive goal, such as going on a trip or doing home renovations, any time the amount of money needed is smaller, you can save it up physically. Using a glass jar to put money in not only sets money aside, but it also acts as a visible source of inspiration and motivation. Every time you put money in your jar, you know that you are moving closer to your goal. Additionally, just seeing the jar can keep your mind focused on the task at hand, giving you the motivation to get started as soon as possible. Thus, even though you might not be able to start the project until you have enough money saved up, by starting the process of setting aside the money, you will essentially have started the project, since you have begun the necessary preparations. In the end, it doesn't matter where or how you start. All that truly matters is that you do start, since once you have started, everything becomes easier as a result.

Create Incentives

The final trick to getting started on any task or project, no matter how large or complex, is to create incentives. Needless to say, such incentives can take many different shapes and forms, each depending on the nature of the task or project you are undertaking. For example, while treating yourself to your favorite ice cream, or a trip to your favorite burger joint may be the perfect reward for writing a chapter in your book or for making headway on a painting project, such a reward is ill-advised if your project is losing weight or starting an exercise regimen. Therefore, it is as important to pick the right reward as it is to create a reward in the first place. In the event you are trying to lose weight, you might choose to reward yourself with clothes shopping when you reach a specific target. Even a simple night out at the movies can go a long way to keeping you on track to reaching your goal.

Another incentive is that of creating accountability. When you are the only person who knows of your goals and dreams, it can be all too easy to put those goals and dreams off for another time. However, when your friends know as well, things suddenly change. Pride can go a long way to helping you stay true to your goals; therefore, it is always good to tell others of the things you want to accomplish. When you tell your friends, they will be sure to ask you about your progress each and every time they see you. Knowing this will keep you motivated to do your best so that you can give them a glowing report when they do ask. Additionally, friends can prove a valuable source of moral support, cheering you on when you need it the most. The positivity they can provide will help to keep your energy at its highest, enabling you to carry on even when you want to quit. Telling friends about a goal will ensure that you get started sooner rather than later, as they will hound you until you do. In the end, even though accountability isn't as nice as a reward, it can be as effective, if not more so when it comes to maintaining motivation and helping you to start that all-important project here and now.

Chapter 9: Bad Habits That Stifle Your Productivity (Plus Productivity Hacks)

Anyone who has ever started a diet, or a healthy life regimen will know that one of the most important aspects of achieving your goal is to break the bad habits and behaviors that are responsible for the situation you want to fix. In other words, before you even think about buying a good pair of running shoes or a mountain of green leafy vegetables, you must first throw away the containers of ice cream and the bags of chips. Only by eliminating the unhealthy foods in the first place can the other measures begin to take effect, helping you to become healthier and happier as a result. The very same thing applies to procrastination. In order for all the tips and tricks to produce the intended results, you must first remove all of the bad habits and behaviors that are keeping you from the success you desire. This chapter will address several of the most common bad habits that stifle your productivity, as well as ways to overcome them once and for all. By the time you finish reading this chapter, you will be able to clear the junk habits out of your life, thereby making way for the healthy, positive habits that will help you to fulfill your true potential.

Multitasking

One of the most common and harmful of all the bad habits regarding productivity is that of multitasking. This is an area where countless people make a critical mistake, one that keeps them from achieving the success they desire. That mistake is to start multiple tasks at once. Although multitasking might sound like you are more productive, the fact of the matter is that it decreases your productivity, making any task take longer to complete than if you had focused on that single task alone. There are actually a couple of reasons why this is the case.

First, there is simple math. If you start one task that will take ten minutes to complete, you can pretty much guarantee that you will get it done in ten minutes' time, provided you don't get distracted or called away. However, if you start five tasks that should only take ten minutes each, you suddenly have a different equation on your hands. Now, instead of getting the one task done in ten minutes, you probably won't get it done for thirty, forty, or even fifty minutes depending on how you split your time between the five different tasks. In the end, instead of speeding up when things get done, multitasking actually pushes back the deadlines, making it less efficient as a result. By focusing on one task at a time, you ensure that each task will be completed in ten minutes from being started, with the end result still being the same, namely getting all five tasks done in fifty minutes.

The second reason why it is better to focus on one task at a time is that you can devote all of your concentration to the task at hand. Numerous studies have shown that when you multitask, it causes your mind to become fragmented, juggling numerous tasks at once rather than simply focusing on one at a time. Furthermore, it has been discovered that the brain can't just go from one task to another seamlessly. Instead, it needs to gear down from one before gearing up for the other. Although it only takes a couple of minutes to switch gears, those minutes can add up over the course of a day, seriously undermining the efficiency of your time. The end result is that when you multitask, it actually takes longer to accomplish the same tasks than if you approached them individually. Therefore, always commit to one task at a time, putting all of your time, effort, and attention into it.

If you have five tasks to address the best approach is to prioritize them, placing the most important and time-sensitive one at the top of the list, while leaving the least important at the bottom. Once your list is made, you can begin performing each item individually, only going on to the next item when the first one is completed in its entirety. Taking a five-minute break between each task will help you to clear your mind and prepare for the next task at hand. Although it seems counter-intuitive in terms of productivity, such breaks will increase the speed and quality of your work, allowing you to produce better results than if you worked straight through. This will keep you organized, fresh, and motivated all throughout the day.

Constantly Focusing on the Big Picture

Another bad habit is that of constantly focusing on the "big picture." This is particularly true in the case of larger projects that require a lot of time and energy to accomplish. As already mentioned, such large projects can cause even the most energetic and hard-working people to procrastinate simply due to their size and scope. Only by breaking down those large projects can a person address them without feeling overwhelmed. However, sometimes it's hard not to remember the big picture, even after the large project has been broken down. This can cause a person to stumble in their progress, feeling overwhelmed, and losing their motivation to carry on.

This situation isn't necessarily the result of a lack of discipline or low self-esteem. Instead, it often happens when a person takes the time to track the progress they are making. The moment their mind leaves the small task at hand and sees the big picture, the feeling of being overwhelmed returns. They suddenly begin to regret taking on such a large project and start to doubt their ability to complete it. Now, instead of being motivated and full of energy, the individual is demoralized and uninspired. These feelings usually cause them to procrastinate on the next step, resulting in the project going unfinished for an indefinite period of time.

Needless to say, contemplating the big picture in any project or task is a necessary step, especially when tracking your progress. The trick is to leave such contemplations for times when you aren't working on the project. In other words, rather than thinking about the big picture while you are working on a specific element of the project, take time at the end of the day to entertain those thoughts. Let your mind focus on the work you are doing while you are doing it and nothing more. This will help to keep you in the zone of the smaller, more manageable task. At the end of the day, you can look at the task as an observer, and this can help to keep you from feeling overwhelmed. Furthermore, by waiting until the end of the day to track your progress, you will always have more progress to show, helping you to stay motivated as you see the big picture getting smaller and smaller by the day.

Being Unstructured

Organization is another key ingredient to improving efficiency and thus increasing productivity. That said, one of the things that keeps most people from fulfilling their true potential is that they are unstructured. This can come in several different forms, including the lack of a work routine, a disorganized workspace, and even a disorganized mindset. In the end, a lack of organization serves to decrease both the amount and the quality of the work that is accomplished. No matter how much time or energy an individual puts into their work, the results will always be modest at best. In short, when a person lacks structure, they lack the direction needed to achieve their goals quickly and successfully.

The lack of a work routine is one of the most significant areas where being unstructured can really have a negative impact. Numerous studies have shown that a person's energy levels fluctuate all throughout the day. Without a work routine, they may wind up sitting idle when their energy levels are at their peak, only to begin tackling the day's tasks when their energy levels are lower, causing them to be less productive as a result. The trick here is to pay attention to when your energy levels are highest, setting aside those times to tackle the hardest, largest tasks during the day. This will ensure that you use your time and energy as efficiently as possible, making you not only more productive but also more motivated, as you will only face demanding tasks when you are full of physical and mental energy.

The same applies to your workspace and mindset. Whenever you have disorganization, it can lead to confusion, time-wasting, and even a lack of inspiration. However, if you take the time to organize your workspace, making it easy to find all of the tools you need for the work you need to do, then you will be able to be more productive as a result. This applies to your mindset, as well. It is critical that you always focus your thoughts and attention on the task at hand. Allowing your mind to wander while you are working not only slows down productivity, it also increases the chances of making costly mistakes that will only make your work even harder. However, when you organize your thoughts, only recognizing those relevant to your work, then you will have a clean and organized mind, one that will be as useful and beneficial as your clean and organized workspace.

Striving for Perfection

Although a seemingly positive concept, perfection can actually prove more harmful than helpful when it comes to productivity. Mainly because our mind will always fixate on the things that can and do go wrong. As a result, the more you focus on perfection, the less likely you are to get anything done. Instead, you will constantly spend your time trying to avoid imperfections or dealing with the imperfections that occur. Since the idea of perfection rarely translates into the real world, it is unlikely that you will achieve perfection no matter how hard you strive to do so.

The inability to achieve perfection can be enough to keep you from getting started on a task if perfection is your aim. The more potential problems you see, the more likely you are to delay or avoid starting a task or project altogether. In the event that you do get started, you will be more likely to quit a project once it becomes clear that achieving a perfect result is beyond reach. Additionally, the stress and fatigue of maintaining unrealistic work standards may prove more than you can handle, causing you to metaphorically "work yourself to death" on a project that would have proven relatively easy otherwise.

Since perfection is a myth, at best, the trick is to not actually waste your time and energy trying to achieve the impossible. Instead, you should focus your attention on finishing each and every task or project you have. The bottom line is that a fully completed project is better than any half-completed one. Even if the half-completed one is perfect, it is still incomplete. In contrast, the finished project is done, meaning it has far greater value despite any flaws or imperfections. If a challenge is what you need, then rather than perfection, try focusing on finishing every task or project ahead of schedule. This will give you that competitive fix while still allowing you to be more productive.

Being Overbooked

Almost everyone feels as though they have more work to do in a given day than they have the time needed to get that work done. While this can prove unavoidable in some cases, more often than not, it is the consequence of another bad habit, specifically, the habit of never saying "no." Most people feel that turning down a request for help or an additional task will somehow appear as a sign of weakness, showing an inability to rise to the challenge. The fear of saying no causes them to constantly take on more and more work, so much so that they wind up getting overbooked. In the end, projects are either late or ignored altogether, making this a vicious cycle that leads to a lack of productivity and the low self-esteem that comes as a result.

The best way to avoid being overbooked is to learn to say "no." Although others may take such a rejection hard at first when you demonstrate your reasons, they will likely come to see the logic behind your decision. Alternatively, instead of simply saying 'no' outright, you might offer to make yourself available once your current task or project is complete. This will help you to put your work first while still proving useful to others when you have the time and energy to spare.

Another highly valuable trick is to schedule time within each and every day to take on additional tasks. Most people fill every single minute of their schedule with work or obligations, allowing no time for extra tasks or tasks that take longer than expected. If you schedule an empty half an hour in the middle or end of your workday, you can either give yourself that extra time for tasks that remain unfinished, or you can devote it to any tasks you take on in an effort to help others. This will ensure that the time you give never undermines your own productivity, thereby eliminating the scenario of being overbooked.

Waiting for Better Conditions

Finally, there is the bad habit of waiting for better conditions. How many times have you put off a task or project because you didn't feel as though you had the right amount of time or energy on hand? This happens to everyone, all of the time. Unfortunately, the right time rarely ever comes, meaning that you keep pushing back a task indefinitely. The same holds true with regard to energy levels. The amount of energy you have today will likely be the same amount of energy you have tomorrow, the next day, and the next day after that. This means that if now isn't the right time, the chances are the right time doesn't actually exist.

In order to break this habit, you need to change the order of things. Rather than shaping your time and energy to the task or project at hand, shape the task or project to the time and energy available. In other words, rather than putting off the entire task for later, simply accomplish as much as you can with the resources you have. Even if you only have ten minutes to spare, and your energy levels are at fifty percent, you will be able to get something done, thereby making more progress than if you did nothing at all. Needless to say, a large task or project may take a while to complete in such circumstances, but at the end of the day, it will get completed, and that's really all that matters. This is how you avoid building that list of huge projects that never get done. By switching things around, you will get every task and project done, no matter how large or labor-intensive they may be.

Chapter 10: The Success Mindset: Five Tips from Success Experts

When it comes to overcoming procrastination, all of the top experts agree on one fundamental truth: change comes from within. Although the methods for overcoming procrastination will help anyone who puts them into practice, in order to achieve true success, it is critical that you change your very way of thinking. The simple fact is that procrastination is usually the result of a failure mindset, the state of mind that focuses on problems, fear of failure, and all the other negative aspects of any endeavor. Alternatively, ambition, inspiration, and a desire to take action are the result of a success mindset, one that is focused on opportunities, dreams, and the rewards that await when goals are achieved. Therefore, in addition to practicing effective time management, organizing your life, and redefining challenges, it is essential that you develop a success mindset in order to realize your full potential and achieve the success you truly crave. This chapter will reveal five proven ways to develop a success mindset, thereby enabling you to overcome procrastination and every other obstacle that has been holding you back from the life you both desire and deserve.

Define Success

One of the most puzzling things to many people is when a seemingly successful person is unhappy with their life. They might have a dream job, a dream house, and the sort of financial security that most people only ever fantasize about, yet in spite of it all, they are still unhappy. To the average person, this might appear to be a sign that they are ungrateful for what they have, that they are unsatisfied with the gains they have achieved. However, the truth of the matter is that they are unhappy because the success they have achieved is not their version of success. Instead, they have achieved what society defines as success. This is where "defining success" plays a crucial role.

In order to be truly successful, you need to decide what success means for you. If it means financial security and all the luxuries that go with it, then pursuing a high paying job may be the path for you to follow. However, success for you might mean freedom, the freedom to do what you want, when you want. Since a high paying job will not afford that kind of freedom, you will need to find another path that will help you to achieve your goal. In the end, chasing after someone else's dream won't bring you happiness. Only when you pursue your dream will you achieve the happy, content life that you desire. Therefore, the first step to creating a success mindset is to sit down and write out the things you want most in life. These are the things that define success for you, and thus they are the things you should pursue in your efforts to turn your dreams into reality.

The next step to defining success is to resolve any inner conflicts that might interfere with the pursuit of your dream. For example, you might dream of getting a high paying job and all the financial stability that comes with it, yet you are afraid that you will sacrifice a happy, loving marriage in the process. This might cause you to drag your feet when it comes to chasing after that dream job. In this case, you need to decide that you can achieve both elements of your dream. By deciding that you will never let your job control your life, you can pursue a path of financial success, while still chasing after love and happiness at home. By addressing the fears and concerns of success, you can take control of your decisions, thus ensuring you achieve true, all-around success.

The final step is to translate your dream into goals. It's not enough to simply decide you want financial security. Instead, you need to determine how to go about achieving that dream. Will you find a high paying job, start a successful business, or make investments that will create your fortune? Needless to say, every destination has many roads leading to it, each from a different angle and perspective. Only by choosing one of these roads can you begin moving in the direction of your dream. Setting goals, both large and small, will help you to lay out a travel plan that you can monitor, thereby tracking your progress and ensuring that your actions and decisions lead you closer to your goal, rather than further away from it.

Create a Growth Mindset

When it comes to creating a success mindset, another factor to take into account is the danger of having a fixed way of thinking. A fixed mindset is when you have a rigid set of beliefs that cannot be changed or altered in any way. More often than not, this fixed set of beliefs includes the things that you consider impossible, faults you feel are a part of your natural condition, and any number of negative aspects that keep you from pursuing your dreams and fulfilling your potential. In contrast, the most successful people create what is known as a growth mindset, one that is capable of changing, evolving, and growing with each and every experience, thereby allowing for the individual to develop their abilities and strengths.

One of the most effective ways to create a growth mindset is to constantly challenge yourself to improve. This is a good way to turn setbacks into learning experiences. Each and every time you experience a setback, rather than admitting defeat, take a look at where you went wrong and determine never to make the same mistakes again. When you achieve this mindset, you eliminate the fear of failure completely from your life, since failure becomes a chance to grow and improve, thereby helping you to hone your skills and pursue your dreams more effectively.

Although failure is a good way to challenge yourself to improve, the most successful people take it a step further and use their successes to challenge growth and development as well. Rather than sitting back and basking in victory, successful people look at their wins and ask how they could have done even better. This constant desire for self-improvement forces you to continually strive to be your best. Even if you fall short of this goal, you will still continue to grow, becoming better with each day and each experience. The trick is to appreciate your achievements, while also looking for ways to make those achievements even better.

Another significant difference between a fixed mindset and a growth mindset is the ability to embrace change. Since change challenges your comfort zone, if you have a fixed mindset, you will resist it at all costs. This means you will never push beyond your accepted limits, resulting in modest levels of success at best. Alternatively, when you have a growth mindset, you will see change as a chance to grow and experience new horizons, horizons that offer fresh opportunities and higher levels of success. By embracing change, not only do you grow, your dreams grow as well, meaning the success you gain by achieving those dreams will be larger than you ever imagined. This growth mindset will take away the fear of the unknown, and thus remove any tendencies toward procrastination that results from such fears.

Become Self-Aware

While the saying: "ignorance is bliss" may be true for some, the fact is that ignorance is usually the cause of failure for most people. This is because the more ignorant you are, the less you know, and the less you know, the less likely you will be to succeed. Knowledge is power, and the most important and powerful of all types of knowledge is that of self-awareness. Only by knowing yourself can you begin to create a success mindset, one that enables you to chase and fulfill all of your dreams and ambitions. Therefore, it is vital that you take the time and effort to become self-aware.

The first step toward becoming self-aware is to discover your weaknesses. This can be a hard process for many, since admitting to your weaknesses is often seen as the same as accepting them. However, the only way you can fix your weaknesses is to know what they are in the first place. Therefore, it is critical that you take the time to contemplate what areas you struggle with. These areas can include anything at all, like public speaking, embracing change, learning new skills, or anything that is outside your comfort zone. Once you discover your weaknesses, you can begin to do two things. First, you can begin to affect change in those areas, developing your skills so that you turn your weaknesses into strengths. The other thing is to make choices that don't expose your weaknesses. In other words, if you struggle with public speaking, then don't necessarily take a job that requires a lot of public speaking, at least not until you take the steps needed to overcome that particular weakness.

The next step is to discover your strengths. This will help you to know what skills you have in abundance, in order to make better decisions all around. If, for example, you are highly skilled at writing, then pursue any opportunity where you can put your writing to use. A big mistake that people make is in assuming that when you tailor your choices to your strengths and weaknesses, you limit your opportunities to those that fall within your comfort zone. In fact, when you tailor your choices in this way, you maximize your chances of success in everything you do. If you never pursue growth and development, then you will run the risk of becoming stagnant. However, you can find a healthy balance where you focus on your strengths, avoid your weaknesses, and continue to improve in all areas. This is one of the keys to achieving both short term and long-term success.

The final step to becoming self-aware is to discover and develop your intuition. Many people shy away from the idea of using intuition when it comes to making important decisions, as it takes away from a more intellectual approach, where data and experience are used to make the best choice. Unfortunately, data and experience aren't always available, meaning that there will be times when your "gut feeling" is your only source of inspiration. By taking the time to develop and listen to your intuition, you gain an advantage, one that allows you to make the best decision, even when there is no empirical data to use in the decision-making process. The trick is to listen to your intuition at all times. Recognize how you feel with each and every decision you make. This will help you to trust your intuition in those times when you have no other source of insight to follow.

Ignore the Opinions of Others

If you've ever listened to the story of a successful person, you will probably have heard them say how they pursued their dreams when others said it couldn't be done. Needless to say, had they paid attention to those negative opinions, they would never have chased their dreams, and thus would never have achieved the success that has since defined them. Therefore, when it comes to creating a success mindset, it is essential that you develop the ability to ignore the opinion of others.

One of the things you need to ignore right away is how others define "success." This goes back to the idea of defining what success means to you personally. All too often, people spend their time and energy pursuing what others perceive as success. Whether it's money, a prestigious job, or any similar common dream, if it's not what you really want, then it will never bring you the happiness you desire. Before you begin chasing a dream, you need to ask yourself who's dream it is that you are chasing. If it's not yours, then it's not right. When you spend your life chasing the dreams of others, you become a slave to their way of thinking. Thus, even if you achieve success, you never actually live your own life. Successful people ignore the vision of success that society shares, choosing to focus on their personal desires and goals, regardless of what others think. In the end, true success is living a life that brings you untold happiness, meaning, and contentment. The only way to achieve such a life is to shut out the vision of success that others hold and focus on your vision, your ambition, and your dreams.

The second opinion to ignore as soon as possible is that of the expectation of failure. Again, how many success stories start with the recollection of how countless people said it couldn't be done? Everything from crossing the ocean to flying to the moon came in spite of almost everyone claiming failure was all but certain. Imagine, for a moment, what the world would be like today had the early explorers and pioneers accepted common belief and simply stayed home, instead of reaching out and achieving greatness. The very same thing holds true for your life. If you allow the negative mindset of others to restrict your vision, then you will only ever achieve the success others can imagine. Alternatively, when you ignore what others say, you open up an infinite world of possibilities, enabling you to pursue any dream as long as you have the ability to envision it and the courage to do what it takes to turn it into reality. In other words, when others tell you that it can't be done, recognize that what they mean is that it can't be done by anyone other than you.

Interestingly enough, another opinion you need to dismiss is that regarding your true worth. It makes sense to ignore people when they tell you something is impossible, as their negativity can hold you back. However, the same thing can happen if you listen to positive people who tell you that you have what it takes to succeed. This isn't to say that you should ignore positive reinforcement completely, rather it means that you shouldn't limit yourself to how others perceive you. Sometimes when other people praise you and hold you in high esteem, it can undermine your willingness to take risks, in order to avoid falling short in their sight. This is what happens when you fall into the trap of upholding other people's expectations. In order to avoid this trap, you need to ignore the opinions of others and focus solely on your goals. Don't worry about how they might react, whether you succeed or fail. Instead, keep your eye on the prize and nothing else. This will enable you to take those chances that you are unsure of, thereby allowing you to expand your horizons and achieve levels of success that others only ever dream of.

Become the Change You Desire

The final element needed to create a success mindset is that of becoming the change you desire. One of the biggest differences between an average person and a successful person is how they perceive change. An average person will believe that the only way they will ever be happy is when the world around them changes. Alternatively, a successful person knows that in order to achieve true happiness and success, they must change their lives, becoming the change they desire. This approach puts happiness within reach by putting you in control of the decisions needed in order to create that happiness.

The first step to creating the change you desire is to visualize what that change looks like. Rather than seeing yourself as you are now, begin to imagine yourself as you want to be. Do you want to be more aggressive and bolder when it comes to making decisions? Do you want to be more at ease when meeting people for the first time? Do you want to be more confident in all areas of your life? In order to achieve these goals, you need to envision what those things look like. See yourself being bolder, more confident, more at ease. What does that look like? Does it change the way you walk, the way you dress, the way you speak? Only when you know what your best self looks like can you begin to make the changes that will transform you from who you are to who you want to be. Therefore, take the time to imagine what your ideal self looks like and write down the qualities of that self. That is the blueprint you will follow to create the life of your dreams.

The next step is to work every single day to develop your ideal self. The bigger the transformation, the more time it will take to achieve. However, each and every day can be an opportunity to focus on one quality and develop it to the max. If you want to appear more confident, focus on your posture, your stride, and how you dress on a day-to-day basis. Constantly look for ways you can improve the things that not only give the appearance of confidence, but which also engender true confidence in your heart and mind. If being more comfortable around people is your goal, then use each and every day to improve your interpersonal skills. Start by simply making eye contact with strangers or those who you want to impress; once you master that then move on to making polite conversation with those same people. By setting small goals on a daily basis, you can achieve transformation gradually, making it more natural and sustainable as a result. The key is to use the opportunities you have to become your ideal self.

The final step to creating the change you desire is to own your shortcomings. Any transformation will take time, and with each success you will face setbacks along the way. Rather than ignoring those setbacks, take the time to own them. Recognize how and why you went wrong. For example, if you fail to make eye contact with the cashier at the coffee shop, embrace the failure. Accept that you failed to take the opportunity to be your best self at that moment. Then ask yourself why it happened. If it was fear, then begin to use the techniques that turn fear into inspiration. Focus on the results of winning as opposed to the results of simply remaining as you are. By embracing your setbacks, you can turn them into learning opportunities, which will give you an even better chance of success the next time around. In the end, a success mindset is all about the direction you are traveling in. Whenever you experience successful results, you know you are on track to achieving your dreams. Whenever you experience setbacks, you know you are off course, and thus not on track to achieving your dreams. Rather than seeing this as a failure, simply see it as an indication that you need to change course, in order to get back to chasing your dreams and thus the happy and successful life you deserve.

Chapter 11: Daily Habits for Motivation and Self-Discipline

When it comes to achieving transformation in your life, there is no magic wand that you can wave to eliminate the bad and bring in the good. Any true change requires vast amounts of time and effort to achieve. This doesn't mean that it has to be difficult, however. In fact, transformation can be relatively easy when approached from the right perspective. The trick is to break down the larger goal into smaller, more manageable goals, just as you would with any large project that you want to accomplish. One of the most effective ways to do this is to create habits that you perform on a daily basis. When you practice behavior that builds motivation and self-discipline each and every day, you will begin to transform your life one day at a time, with each result building on the last. In the course of thirty, sixty, or ninety days, the changes in the way you think and act will be nothing short of remarkable. This chapter will explore eight habits that will help create the motivation and self-discipline you need to overcome procrastination once and for all, thus enabling you to live the productive, meaningful life you are capable of.

Wake Up at a Decent Hour

The first and perhaps most important of all daily habits to form is that of waking up at a decent hour. One of the biggest mistakes most people make is that they sleep in until the very last minute, before jumping out of bed and rushing around getting ready for the day ahead. This starts the morning in a state of stress and panic, creating a negative mindset that will define the rest of the day. In order to avoid this stress and panic, it is vital that you wake up at a decent hour every day.

In addition to giving you more time to get ready, waking up at an early hour will also give you the chance to spend some quality time doing what you want to do. You might choose to go for a run, read the newspaper, catch up on social media, or simply savor a cup of your favorite coffee beverage. This act of spending time for yourself will put you in a better frame of mind all day, making you feel more important and more in control. The lack of stress and chaos will help increase your motivation for the day ahead, and the act of getting up at a set time will instill a sense of self-discipline, which will help you to take charge of all your decisions and actions for the rest of the day.

This habit needs to be performed every single day, including your days off. A bad habit that many people fall into is that of sleeping in on their days off. All this does is make it harder to wake up earlier on ordinary days. The bottom line is that your body is programmable. Therefore, it works best when it has a set, consistent routine. Changing your morning routine from one day to the next only confuses your body, adding stress to both your body and mind. Thus, practice your morning routine every single day in order to get the best results.

Perform a Small Task First Thing in the Morning

When you wake up at a decent time, it is important that you don't simply waste that extra time. Instead, it is vital that you use it to perform tasks that will help build motivation and self-discipline, and thus help you to stay in control all throughout the day. One such task might be to make your bed when you get up. Numerous studies have shown that when you make your bed first thing in the morning, it goes a long way to creating a positive mindset that will keep you motivated all day long. The reason for this is that the act of making your bed is something that benefits you and you alone. Performing a task for your benefit first thing in the morning has the effect of making you the most important person in your mind. Rather than serving your job or some other entity, it serves your wellbeing. This will help you to stay motivated as you have a higher sense of self-esteem and self-worth.

Another benefit of performing a task, such as making your bed first thing, is that it establishes self-discipline. Instead of sitting in front of the TV or turning on social media, you choose to perform a chore. This puts things into proper perspective, allowing you to keep your priorities in order. Additionally, the act of making your bed serves to keep your environment clean and organized. This will impact your state of mind, helping you to be organized in both thoughts and actions all throughout the day. Furthermore, at the end of the day when you come home, you will find your space more inviting, as it is neat and clean. This will help you to unwind more, thereby getting better rest and feeling more restored the next morning.

Visualize Your Dream

After you have performed your early morning task, the next thing you should do each day is visualize your dream. This doesn't mean contemplating all of the things you need to do in order to achieve your dream. Rather, this is the act of visualizing the big picture, the image of where you want to be, the success you crave, and the rewards you will enjoy once you turn your dream into reality. In other words, this is about visualizing the destination, not the journey.

The best way to visualize your dream is to use a visual tool, such as a vision board. As already discussed, a vision board can be covered with photos and other objects that help you to picture living the life of your dreams. Vision boards are one of the most effective tools for this purpose, but you can use any photo or item to achieve the same result. The important thing is that you spend a few quality minutes each morning focusing on your dream, so that you increase your motivation for the day ahead.

Another critical benefit that comes from visualizing your dream is that it can go a long way to keeping you in a positive mindset, no matter how your day unfolds. This is particularly true in the event that you hate your job. By focusing on your dream in the morning, you remind yourself that your present difficulties are temporary and that they may actually be serving a necessary function, one that helps you to move closer to your goals. This will keep everything in perspective, thereby helping you to transcend any stress or difficulties that rise up during the day.

Visualize Your Day

The next habit to form in your early morning hours is to visualize your day. This is a more practical exercise, one that helps you to organize and plan the day ahead. Instead of picturing your overall dream, this exercise will simply help you to visualize how you want your day to unfold. On the one hand, you can choose to visualize yourself being productive, accomplishing everything you need to that day. You can use this time to create a mental schedule of sorts, one that helps you to stay on track with your efforts all day long. This helps to increase your self-discipline by instilling a sense of purpose and direction, rather than letting you simply get caught up in the momentum of the day.

On the other hand, you might choose to visualize your day in terms of the energy you want to maintain as your day unfolds. In other words, you might visualize yourself being calm and collected in spite of any chaos surrounding you. Or you might visualize yourself as you interact with others, imagining yourself as being confident, engaging, and capable of getting your point across to everyone you talk to. The more you rehearse your day mentally, the more likely you are to put on your best performance, thus ensuring you have a good day every day.

Write Down a Task List

Visualizing your day can help to remind you of the things you want to accomplish on any given day. This leads to the next habit: writing down a task list in the morning. A task list doesn't have to be extensive—consisting of a dozen or more items that will ensure you don't get a moment to breathe before the day is done. Instead, it can consist of as few as three or four items that simply need to be accomplished within a given timeframe. The point of this exercise is twofold. First, it helps you to never forget the things you need to do by writing them down and referring to your list throughout the day. This helps to raise your productivity as well as reduce the stress caused by forgetting important tasks or errands.

Secondly, it helps you to increase your ability to recognize and remember the tasks that need to be done. By creating a list, you become more disciplined in your mindset, focusing on the important issues rather than simply allowing your thoughts to wander in any direction at all. In a way, creating a task list helps you to keep your mind focused and sharp, thereby giving you the mental self-discipline that most people lack. Your list will also make your day purpose-driven, which will help to keep you motivated and on track when others lose their drive and simply drift along.

Cross off Each Item as You Accomplish It

Once you have created your list, the next step is to begin accomplishing the tasks on it. The thing most people forget and the next habit you need to form is to cross off each item as you accomplish it. There are three main reasons why this is vital for increasing both self-discipline and motivation. First, by crossing off the items on your list, you give your list importance. If you only look at your list a couple of times a day, it will become harder and harder to keep writing it each day. It's like if you write grocery lists but always forget to take them with you when you go shopping. Eventually, you would stop making those lists since the effort would seem wasted. However, when you use your list, then the effort is validated, and it keeps you motivated to keep writing them.

The second reason why you should cross off items as you accomplish them is to help you to maintain a sense of control over your day. Rather than bouncing around from one thing to another, you have a clear direction to follow. Each time you check off an item, you remind yourself of that direction, as well as the fact that you are staying on course to achieving your goals.

Finally, there is the element of motivation. As you check off one item after another, you will build a sense of achievement, and this will help to maintain your motivation at the highest level. By the end of the day, as you check off that last item on your list, you will feel as though your day was well spent. By tracking your progress, you show just how productive you are, and this builds self-confidence and self-esteem. Therefore, instead of just meandering through each day, make sure you write a list of what you want to accomplish, big or small, and cross those items off as you go to reap the rewards.

Take Time to Reflect at the End of the Day

All successful people practice the habit of taking time to reflect at the end of the day. As little as ten minutes can go a long way to transforming your life from one of mediocrity to one of confidence, purpose, and success. The trick here is to set aside a specific time in the evening when you can be alone with your thoughts. During this time, recollect the events of the day, both good and bad. In the case of the bad events, ask yourself what went wrong and why. This isn't about self-criticism or self-loathing, rather it's about learning the lessons that setbacks can teach. If you made a mistake in how you handled a situation, recognize that mistake and determine to never repeat it. You can take this time to imagine how you could have handled the situation better, and then you can take that and apply it to your visualization practice the next morning. This is how you make steady and meaningful progress, the progress that enables you to transform your life in a real and significant way.

In the case of good events, you can take this time to relive your moments of triumph and glory. After all, it is important to celebrate each and every win, no matter how large or small. By taking the time to recall the good moments, you raise your motivation levels by recognizing your achievements. This will help you to make the right choices each and every time, thus ensuring you are your best self every single day. You can even take the time to congratulate yourself on a job well done, something that will go a long way to making you feel good about yourself. The important thing is to use this time to track your progress in terms of self-improvement. Although some days will be bad, others will be wonderful. The goal is to have your wonderful days far outnumber your bad ones.

Go to Bed at a Decent Hour

The final habit that will help you to achieve the success you both desire and deserve, is to always go to bed at a decent hour. Sleep deprivation is a common condition in the Western world. One reason for this is that many people stay up late to watch TV in an attempt to unwind from a stressful day. Unfortunately, by staying up late, they wake up tired, and this leads to even more stress and fatigue the next day. Thus, staying up late creates a vicious cycle that only serves to undermine a person's overall health and wellbeing.

By going to bed at a decent hour, you ensure you will get the sleep you need to fully recharge your batteries, both physically and mentally. This will help you to get an early start in order to establish self-discipline throughout your day. Furthermore, the more rested you are, the more energy you will have, and this will increase your motivation as well as your overall performance all day long. Therefore, while unwinding may seem like a good solution, the fact is that getting the right amount of sleep each night is the best option to take good care of your body and mind.

Additionally, once you create a regular sleep routine, your body will respond, and this will ensure that the quality of sleep you get is the absolute best. As mentioned earlier, your body is programmable. Therefore, it will respond far better when you practice the discipline of going to bed and waking up at the same time every day, than if you change your sleep pattern from one day to the next. In the end, that is why habits are so effective. As you practice habits on a daily basis, you reprogram your mind and body, and this allows you to transform your life from the one you have to the one you want. The key is to replace the bad habits that have been holding you back with the good ones that will help you to fulfill your dreams.

Chapter 12: Relapse Is Not the End of the World

This book has provided all the tools and insights you need in order to develop the behaviors and habits that will enable you to eliminate procrastination and laziness from your life. Unfortunately, the chances are you will experience setbacks along the way, specifically in terms of relapses into your old way of thinking and acting. The important thing here is to realize two vital things. First, this isn't a pass or fail scenario; therefore, it is critical that you eliminate the "all or nothing" mindset when it comes to transforming your life. Even the strongest and most determined people experience relapses; therefore, you are not alone, nor are you a failure because of it. The second thing to realize is that a relapse isn't the end of the world. Just because you have a bad day or fall back into lazy habits doesn't mean that the journey is over. A good way to think of it is like getting a flat tire on a road trip. If you get a flat tire, it doesn't mean you have to cancel your road trip and return home. All it means is that you need to fix your tire and get back on the road as soon as possible. This chapter will reveal some of the ways you can get back on the road when you experience a relapse into procrastination or laziness. By practicing these methods, you can ensure that you overcome each and every setback, continuing your journey to creating the life of your dreams.

Embrace the Setbacks

The first trick if you experience a relapse is to embrace the setback. All too often, people jump to a negative mindset in the face of a relapse, one that is full of self-criticism and shame. In the end, such a mindset only makes matters worse, often undermining self-confidence and motivation. Therefore, the best approach to any setback or relapse is to embrace it as a learning experience. See what you can learn from it and how you can grow stronger as a result.

One lesson that relapses often teach us is the value of self-care. Sometimes what causes the relapse is exhaustion or mental fatigue. This usually happens when you become too productive in your attempt to overcome procrastination and laziness. Such relapses can be a sign that your mind needs a break. In a way, it's the same situation as when your body becomes sick due to being overworked and not having enough rest. Therefore, it may be that you need to give yourself a break and take a few days off to rest and restore your energies. The chances are that after a few days you will be ready and eager to get back to your usual routine, thus proving that the setback was actually a positive experience and nothing to feel guilty about.

Another cause of a relapse is the simple lack of motivation. This can happen when you feel stuck in a rut, where your efforts aren't producing results that inspire happiness or satisfaction. In this case, the trick is to change up your routine, adding something completely new and different. Starting a new exercise regimen could jump-start your motivation, or maybe picking up a new hobby or interest will help. In the end, your relapse might just be a sign that you are tired of doing the same old thing day in and day out. Introducing a new experience or direction might be the key to getting you out of that rut and back on track to personal transformation.

In the event that a relapse is long-lasting or that you experience numerous relapses back to back, it might be an indication that the approach you are taking is not necessarily the best one for you. Taking some time to come up with a different plan is a good way to make use of a relapse, turning it into an opportunity to improve your situation overall. By coming up with a new plan, you can shift the responsibility for the relapse from you to the tools you are using. This will remove the guilt and shame that relapses can cause. Additionally, it will help to inspire you to move forward once again. Simply trying the same method over and over again will undermine your motivation if that method keeps failing. However, when you change the method, you give yourself a fresh hope, one that will give you the confidence you need to get back into the proverbial race.

Learn to Celebrate the Positives

The second trick to overcoming relapses is to celebrate the positives. One of the things about the process of self-transformation is that it is continual. You never actually reach a point where you feel as though you have made all the changes you want to make. The fact is that with each change, you discover new possibilities, and those possibilities become your next set of goals. From time to time, the constant, never-ending effort may catch up with you, causing you to feel as though you are getting nowhere. That is why taking the time to celebrate the positives can go a long way in helping you to overcome your setbacks.

One way to do this is to refer to your journal. As mentioned in this book, it is vital that you keep a journal to not only list out your goals but to also track your progress. By sitting down and reviewing your journal, you can see all of the goals you have accomplished and all the changes you have made in your life. This will show you how much progress you have made and how much your efforts have paid off. In a way, it comes down to the fact that every race has two lines, a starting line, and a finish line. When you get fixated on the fact that you haven't reached the finish line, you can become distressed and uninspired. However, if you take a moment to see how far you have come from the starting line, suddenly you see things from a different perspective. Sure, you might not be done with the race yet, but you have come a long way since you started, and that's really all that matters in the end.

Keeping track of your relapses is another way to actually stay on top of them. The simple truth is that relapses will happen, and they will happen more than once. It's a lot like accidents in the workplace. No matter how careful and conscientious people are, there will always be accidents from time to time. The trick is to make those accidents as few and far between as possible. Keeping a count of the number of days between accidents is a common practice in the workplace, showing employees how effective their efforts have been. It also serves as a motivator to keep them at their best so that the number can grow larger and larger. Counting the days between relapses can have the same effect on your motivation and sense of accomplishment. The fact is that the stronger you become, the less frequent your relapses will be. When you see the number of days growing larger between each setback, you can take pride in the progress you have made, despite the setback itself. This is how you turn a failure into a success and it's one of the most effective ways to maintain motivation, even in the hardest of times.

Seek Out Fresh Motivation

The final trick to overcoming relapses is to recharge your motivation batteries. Sometimes the things that motivated you at first become stale, resulting in them having less of an impact when it comes to inspiring you to be your best. This isn't a failure of yours, nor is it a sign that you can't accomplish your goal. Instead, it simply means that it's time for you to seek out fresh motivation. By replacing the old, worn-out quotes and memes with a fresh batch, you can rediscover the spark that enables you to forge ahead along the path of self-transformation.

One option is to watch something that motivates you. This can be anything from motivational speeches and seminars to movies that inspire you. The important thing is to find what works best for you and use that approach. If a Tony Robbins video is what gets your blood pumping, then watch one or more of them. However, if watching a movie where the main character overcomes all the odds and achieves the impossible is where you find your inner strength, then watch a few of those. Take the time to really feed your mind with fresh motivation before getting back into your day-to-day routine. This is another way of embracing the setback and using it to your advantage.

Sometimes all you need to overcome a setback is a good, strong dose of encouragement. This is why it is vital to create a support group in your life, one comprised of friends or family who can provide encouragement, advice, or just a good, strong dose of positive energy to help you get out of your rut. Taking a little time off to spend with your support group can go a long way to recharging your batteries and giving you the boost you need to jumpstart your transformation once again. In fact, your support group might be able to offer insights as to why you are struggling in the first place. One of the best things about an effective support group is that it prevents you from ever feeling as though you are all alone. Rather than having to achieve your transformation single-handedly, you can rely on the help, advice, and support of others to push past the obstacles and reach your ultimate destination—creating the life of your dreams.

Conclusion

Now that you have read *Procrastination: Discover How to Cure Laziness, Overcome Bad Habits, Develop Motivation, Improve Self-Discipline, Adopt a Success Mindset, and Increase Productivity, Even If You Are a Lazy Person*, you have all the insights and tools you need to begin eliminating procrastination from your life in every way possible. From addressing the emotional and psychological causes that keep you from pursuing your goals to overcoming the bad habits that undermine your productivity, you will be able to start accomplishing any task or project you set your mind to. Additionally, by introducing good habits into your day-to-day life, you can begin to transform your life, using each and every day to create the life of your dreams. Finally, when you begin to replace lazy habits and tendencies with productive, purpose-driven habits and tendencies, you will begin to develop higher levels of self-confidence and self-esteem, thereby improving your life in every way imaginable. In short, by practicing the methods and techniques in this book, you will discover and fulfill your true potential, thus becoming your ideal self. Good luck on your journey to achieving the success you both desire and deserve!

Here's another book by Deon Hillman that you might like

Sources

https://www.youtube.com/watch?v=7DvftaHlZR0

https://www.developgoodhabits.com/causes-of-procrastination/

https://www.psychologicalscience.org/observer/why-wait-the-science-behind-procrastination

https://www.youtube.com/watch?v=TY3k4KbpuUg

https://www.psychologytoday.com/intl/blog/fulfillment-any-age/201204/the-paradox-procrastination

https://www.youtube.com/watch?v=gd7wAithl7I

https://academichelp.net/uncategorized/differences-procrastination-and-laziness.html

https://incredibleplanet.net/the-difference-between-laziness-and-procrastination/

https://www.youtube.com/watch?v=9_gu7e5L-wg

http://yourpositivitycoach.com/why-negative-thoughts-create-discouragement-and-lack-of-motivation/

https://www.youtube.com/watch?v=dopb3jBlrXc

https://www.psychologytoday.com/us/blog/dont-delay/201803/how-negative-thoughts-relate-procrastination

https://www.developgoodhabits.com/mental-models/

https://www.youtube.com/watch?v=wmx_35rQIRg

https://www.youtube.com/watch?v=adDgQeRavzU

https://www.youtube.com/watch?v=OQLdyPuF6ig

https://gettingthingsdone.com/2017/04/10-tips-for-success-with-gtd/

https://dev.to/duomly/10-tips-to-increase-your-productivity-and-get-things-done-3n3e

https://thezeroed.com/steps-effective-goal-setting/

https://www.makeuseof.com/tag/start-project-now-dont-feel-like/

https://www.youtube.com/watch?v=3-embFrOVL4

https://www.developgoodhabits.com/bad-productivity-habits/

https://www.acquirent.com/what-is-a-success-mindset/

https://www.youtube.com/watch?v=1vIvnNEyB-w

https://www.youtube.com/watch?v=MmfikLimeQ8

https://www.youtube.com/watch?v=-71zdXCMU6A

https://gregandfionascott.com/success-mindset-2/

https://thriveglobal.com/stories/5-steps-to-develop-a-success-mindset/

https://www.lifeoptimizer.org/2017/04/06/motivation-vs-self-discipline-habit-formation/

https://medium.com/personal-growth-lab/6-daily-habits-to-make-motivation-flow-effortlessly-c4156661e221

https://vocal.media/motivation/10-methods-to-improve-self-discipline

https://www.positivityblog.com/how-to-stop-being-so-lazy/

https://stephaniepollock.com/5-helpful-project-steps/

https://www.livescience.com/20026-brain-dopamine-worker-slacker.html

https://www.achieve-goal-setting-success.com/personality.html,

https://www.lifereaction.com/great-goal-setting-personality-type/

https://www.youtube.com/watch?v=54aFTZ9POw4,

https://www.tlnt.com/6-reasons-not-to-use-smart-goals-for-everything/

https://www.employeeconnect.com/blog/difference-between-core-values-mission-vision-statements-and-goals/

https://www.greycampus.com/blog/project-management/personal-vision-mission-statement-how-do-you-build-them

https://www.youtube.com/watch?v=Lp_GOrM16Xc

https://www.youtube.com/watch?v=mBLGngFI5Ec

https://www.youtube.com/watch?v=BzAaOgzjPik,

https://www.youtube.com/watch?v=GOfl2sbgPhk

https://www.youtube.com/watch?v=WEaHtroHuoU

https://www.youtube.com/watch?v=EBgugeKaJa8

https://www.thelazygeniuscollective.com/blog/goals

https://medium.com/accelerated-intelligence/if-you-want-to-be-massively-successful-do-not-set-ambitious-goals-according-to-studies-affa9cd39f5d

https://www.bolde.com/lazy-girls-guide-setting-goals/

https://www.youtube.com/watch?v=RlGQsAX7q8w,

https://www.mindmeister.com/blog/mind-mapping-benefits-who-needs-mind-maps/

https://productivityland.com/best-mind-mapping-software/

https://blog.mindvalley.com/vision-board/

https://www.tinypulse.com/blog/10-ways-to-meet-your-goals-with-time-management

https://www.entrepreneur.com/article/299336

https://www.holstee.com/blogs/mindful-matter/three-ways-reflection-can-influence-your-goals

https://www.pickthebrain.com/blog/top-5-reasons-reviewing-goals-must-success/

https://www.sparringmind.com/good-habits/

https://medium.com/personal-growth-lab/6-daily-habits-to-make-motivation-flow-effortlessly-c4156661e221

http://www.motivade.com/blog/2013/08/how-to-stay-motivated-daily/